ADRIAN HENRI

Collected Poems 1967–85

A·H. 56

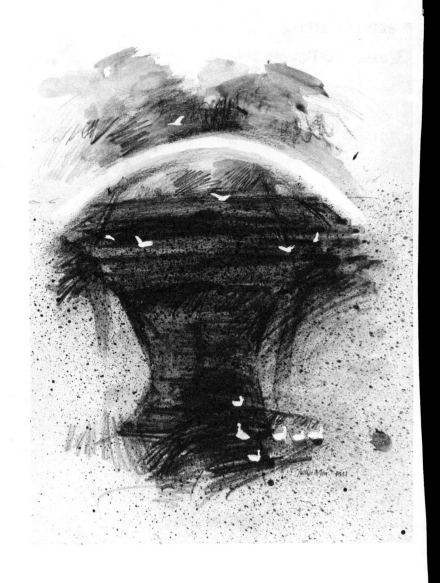

ADRIAN HENRI

Collected Poems 1967–85

drawings by Adrian Henri

ALLISON & BUSBY

LONDON   NEW YORK

First published in Great Britain 1986 by
Allison & Busby Limited
6a Noel Street, London W1V 3RB
and distributed in the USA by
Schocken Books Inc.
62 Cooper Square, New York 10003

Collected Poems 1967–85 is published simultaneously in a
paperback edition, a hardback edition, and also in a specially
bound edition autographed by the author and limited to
eighty copies

British Library Cataloguing in Publication Data

Henri, Adrian
    Collected poems 1967–85
    I. Title
    821'.914   PR6058.E53

    ISBN 0–85031–655–3
    ISBN 0–85031–656–1 Pbk
    ISBN 0–85031–758–4 Ltd Ed

Book design: John Latimer Smith

Photoset in 10/12pt Palatino by
Ann Buchan (Typesetters), Walton-on-Thames, Surrey
Printed and bound in Great Britain by
Richard Clay (The Chaucer Press) Ltd, Bungay, Suffolk

Contents

Introduction

This book contains all my poems printed in book form between 1967 and 1983, plus some unpublished work and poems printed only in anthologies or limited editions: most of the work has been out of print for some time.

I have kept the work in roughly chronological sequence, so that it forms a sort of life-story over twenty years, as well as showing changing interests in forms and subjects. Most of the poems are more or less autobiographical, and in many cases dedicated to friends or lovers. This is no place to add a long list of further dedications; where these don't appear I hope the original recipients will take this as read. It would be impossible to thank all the many people without whose friendship and hospitality the travel poems published here couldn't have been written.

Inevitably, my early training and continuing work as a painter has affected my writing, and vice versa. The occasional visuals I've added are meant to be a sort of parallel commentary on my work in that area. Anyone interested in seeing more might look at the catalogue of *The Art of Adrian Henri, 1955–1985* (South Hill Park, Bracknell 1986).

"Tonight at Noon and Other Poems" comprises work from *The Liverpool Scene* (Rapp and Carroll 1967), *Penguin Modern Poets No. 10: The Mersey Sound* (Penguin 1967 and 1974), *Love Love Love* (Corgi 1967), *Tonight at Noon* (Rapp and Whiting 1986) and *The Best of Henri* (Jonathan Cape 1975), plus two unpublished poems from 1960–61, "Death of a Bird in the City" and "Piccadilly Poems". "City" was published by Rapp and Whiting in 1969. "America" was written in 1969–70, and published by Turret Books in 1972. "Haiku" was privately printed for me for New Year 1975. The rest of the book comes from the following volumes published by Jonathan Cape: *Autobiography* (1971), *City Hedges* (1977), *From the Loveless Motel* (1980) and *Penny Arcade* (1983).

All enquiries for permission to reprint these works should be addressed to my agents, Deborah Rogers Ltd, 49 Blenheim Crescent, London W 11.

ADRIAN HENRI

TONIGHT AT NOON
& OTHER POEMS

Me

if you weren't you, who would you like to be?

Paul McCartney Gustav Mahler
Alfred Jarry John Coltrane
Charlie Mingus Claude Debussy
Wordsworth Monet Bach and Blake

Charlie Parker Pierre Bonnard
Leonardo Bessie Smith
Fidel Castro Jackson Pollock
Gaudi Milton Munch and Berg

Belà Bartók Henri Rousseau
Rauschenberg and Jasper Johns
Lukas Cranach Shostakovich
Kropotkin Ringo George and John

William Burroughs Francis Bacon
Dylan Thomas Luther King
H.P. Lovecraft T.S. Eliot
D.H. Lawrence Roland Kirk

Salvatore Giuliano
Andy Warhol Paul Cézanne
Kafka Camus Ensor Rothko
Jacques Prévert and Manfred Mann

Marx Dostoievsky
Bakunin Ray Bradbury
Miles Davis Trotsky
Stravinsky and Poe

Danilo Dolci Napoleon Solo
St John of the Cross and
The Marquis de Sade

Charles Rennie Mackintosh
Rimbaud Claes Oldenburg
Adrian Mitchell and Marcel Duchamp

James Joyce and Hemingway
Hitchcock and Buñuel
Donald McKinlay Thelonius Monk

Alfred, Lord Tennyson
Matthias Grünewald
Philip Jones Griffiths and Roger McGough

Guillaume Apollinaire
Cannonball Adderley
René Magritte
Hieronymus Bosch

Stéphane Mallarmé and Alfred de Vigny
Ernst Mayakovsky and Nicolas de Staël
Hindemith Mick Jagger Dürer and Schwitters
Garcia Lorca
                and
                    last of all
                        me.

Tonight at Noon*

(for Charles Mingus and the Clayton Squares)

Tonight at noon
Supermarkets will advertise 3d EXTRA on everything
Tonight at noon

2

Children from happy families will be sent to live in a home
Elephants will tell each other human jokes
America will declare peace on Russia
World War I generals will sell poppies in the streets on
    November 11th
The first daffodils of autumn will appear
When the leaves fall upwards to the trees

Tonight at noon
Pigeons will hunt cats through city backyards
Hitler will tell us to fight on the beaches and on the landing
    fields
A tunnel full of water will be built under Liverpool
Pigs will be sighted flying in formation over Woolton
and Nelson will not only get his eye back but his arm as well
White Americans will demonstrate for equal rights
in front of the Black House
and the Monster has just created Dr Frankenstein

Girls in bikinis are moonbathing
Folksongs are being sung by real folk
Artgalleries are closed to people over 21
Poets get their poems in the Top 20
Politicians are elected to insane asylums
There's jobs for everyone and nobody wants them
In back alleys everywhere teenage lovers are kissing
in broad daylight

In forgotten graveyards the dead will quietly bury the living
and
You will tell me you love me
Tonight at noon.

*The title for this poem is taken from an LP by Charlie Mingus, *Tonight At
    Noon*.

Death of a Bird in the City II

(for Philip Jones Griffiths and his photographs)

Guns are bombarding Piccadilly
Firing at ten million splattered white dying birds

Doors thrown open
Girls mouths screaming
The last unbearable white bird
Spotlit, slowly struggling threshing against blackness
Crucified on the easel
SCHWEPPES
GUINNESS IS . . .
The lights are going out . . .
A blind old woman with light running from her glasses
Seeing nothing.
The plaster Christ has got up and is kneeling before the plaster
    donkey

Buildings are falling silently
Neonsigns are running like blood
The COCA-COLA sun is setting
The plaster Mary following the star
B.P.   MAX FACTOR
To where the Three Kings lay
The last bird has leapt weeping
Onto the neon wheel
Delicious
REFRESHING
Screaming through the echoing ruins of Piccadilly
Under the bombardment of the night.

Adrián Ituarte
De amiga Buá
in the City
1986

Piccadilly Poems

1

Piccadilly
Vast overflowing abundances of poemness
LEWIS'S
. . . THE NATIONAL BANK
A bus 83a O God in my mind screaming
dragged beneath the wheels
Horatory
Minatory
Messianic
the ghost of Guillaume Apollinaire
watches from glass and concrete perspectives of bus stations.

2

DAFFODILS ARE NOT REAL!

3

Sitting in a city square in the April sunshine
I see the first beachheads of the Martian invasion
Lapping over the rusticated walls.

4

7 cowboys stride into the city
Hitch their horses to a bus terminal
Sun on their shirts sweat on their faces dust caking their jeans
Gun resting easily on hip.

6

5

NIGHT the time of the terrible neon wheel.

6

The smell of grass being mowed in the square;
I sit in a café in Piccadilly
And think of Yves Tanguy
Alone in the crowded dugout eating sandwiches full of
    spiders.

Without You

Without you every morning would be like going back to work
    after a holiday,
Without you I couldn't stand the smell of the East Lancs Road,
Without you ghost ferries would cross the Mersey manned by
    skeleton crews,
Without you I'd probably feel happy and have more money
    and time and nothing to do with it,
Without you I'd have to leave my stillborn poems on other
    people's doorsteps, wrapped in brown paper,
Without you there'd never be sauce to put on sausage butties,
Without you plastic flowers in shop windows would just be
    plastic flowers in shop windows
Without you I'd spend my summers picking morosely over
    the remains of train crashes,
Without you white birds would wrench themselves free from
    my paintings and fly off dripping blood into the night,
Without you green apples wouldn't taste greener,
Without you Mothers wouldn't let their children play out after
    tea,

7

Without you every musician in the world would forget how to
   play the blues,
Without you Public Houses would be public again,
Without you the Sunday Times colour supplement would
   come out in black-and-white,
Without you indifferent colonels would shrug their shoulders
   and press the button,
Without you they'd stop changing the flowers in Piccadilly
   Gardens,
Without you Clark Kent would forget how to become
   Superman,
Without you Sunshine Breakfast would only consist of Corn-
   flakes,
Without you there'd be no colour in Magic colouring books,
Without you Mahler's 8th would only be performed by street
   musicians in derelict houses,
Without you they'd forget to put the salt in every packet of
   crisps,
Without you it would be an offence punishable by a fine of up
   to £200 or two months' imprisonment to be found in
   possession of curry powder,
Without you riot police are massing in quiet sidestreets,
Without you all streets would be one-way the other way,
Without you there'd be no one not to kiss goodnight when we
   quarrel,
Without you the first martian to land would turn round and go
   away again,
Without you they'd forget to change the weather,
Without you blind men would sell unlucky heather,
Without you there would be
no landscapes/no stations/no houses,
no chipshops/no quiet villages/no seagulls
on beaches/no hopscotch on pavements/no night/no
   morning/there'd be no city no country
Without you.

Fairground Poem

My mind is a fairground
Noise-Gaiety-Bright
colours, at the back
THE VAMPIRES CAVE
huge bats with horrible
wings like old umbrellas
(but the vampires are really fruitbats
and live on old mouldy peaches the punters won't buy)
And the FUN HOUSE with the beautiful dark-eyed Madonna
who smiles at me but is married to someone else
And pimply girls in cowboy hats
THE CISCO KID emerge and lascivious compressed air blows up
    their skirts
(sometimes they cross this part three or four times)
Beautiful little girls of 12 or 13 in enormous sunglasses
With beautiful tight little arses
(like two plums in a wet paper bag)
and firm little tits like toffee apples 6d.
she smiles at me sexily (holding her mother's
arm) her mouth bursting with little even teeth,
knowing I want to have her and can't
(*"Don't be a burke, you'd get your collar felt"*)
And always in my mind echoes of false promises:
    YOU CAN PICK WHAT YOU LIKE
    Just one over to win
    Come here dear I'm going to treat you today
    I'll tell you what I'll do for you
    Come here, luv, no money. . . .
    Just get one in. . . .
    PICK WHAT YOU LIKE
    ANY PRIZE YOU LIKE
    Roll 'em down and add 'em up
    If you come from WIGAN
    You can 'ave a BIG 'UN
And at the back where there's still a headache
from Bitter and Younger's and pills yesterday

the carriages bump ahead in mysterious Ghost Train darkness
Screaming at painted horrors
Washleather ghostly fingers
polythene skeletons
hand slides carefully up warm nylon to warm dampness at top
In the brief intimacy
Then the sudden blinding reality
All out quickly
Pay again if you want to stay on
Bright lights smell of onions doughnuts frankfurters
My mind is crammed with stupid questions:

> *What will you give us if we lose?*
> *What do you 'ave to do, Mister, to win?*
> *'ow much am they?*

My mind is easily corrupted
Grateful to be fed on

> Candyfloss
> Hamburgers
> Brandysnaps
> Toffeeapples
> Cheeseburgers
> DO-NUTS

My mind is pathetically grateful for small worthless gifts

> Cinderella watches
> Glass Ashtrays
> Miniature playing kards
> polythene dolls
> Plaster Alsatians (*would you like it standing up or lying down, dear?*)
> kazoos that don't play
> Magic Painting Books
> Glass Milk Jugs
> Sets of glasses
> Plastic cars with no wheels

While my mind dreams of possessing huge cuddly red and
  yellow rabbits
and glittering canteens of cutlery
My mind is thrown about whirling on the FIGURE EIGHT

10

COASTER, WALTZER, OCTOPUS, Jumping galloping horses THE
   MAD MOUSE
Deafened by music from all sides
  Johnny, remember . . .
  She's a square,
  Baby, I don't care. . . .
And every day the newspaper headlines get worse
and I know that one day they'll get really bad
   KHRUSHCHEV RAPES JACKIE KENNEDY
and then the old man wil l shuffle up an hour or two later
With his horrible smile and say
Late extra, sir – 5 o'clock winner?
  And I'll see the headlines
   WAR DECLARED
And I'll give away all the prizes
take all the money out of the till
rush over to the awful dirty club kept by the horrible old
   woman across the road
put all my money on the counter
and wait.

April Message

"Pack up. Your situation is untenable, your loss irretrievable
    Y no hay remedio. CHANGE YOUR BEDDING!" – Palinurus

"Mr Henri's April Message will be a little late this year"

1

"April" he told us with something approaching confidence
" is the cruellest month." "That's as may be"
I thought
Remembering at least one April when I was happy
Thinking of salads blossoming on city tables
Of someone flying to Canada
leaving behind a sadfaced monkey to be looked after by his
    friends
April
When suicides blossom on bridges
Unquiet dead washed by the sea on beaches
Businessmen tread quietly through art galleries
lest they disturb the nymph sleeping by the sacred fountain
Or the beautiful lady with the face made of flowers
Sydney Carton changes his mind at the last minute
and takes to his heels down the nearest boulevard
muttering "it is a far far better thing I do. . . ."
They're putting your head on the cupwinners medals this year
April
    Turning night into May.

2

Country Poem

Owls were hooting when I went to bed
And when I got up blackbirds were singing
and I hadn't slept at all in between
Thinking about you.

12

3

Liverpool Love Poem

I love you
You love me
   Ee-ay-addio
     You
       love
         me.

4

Clouds
      tumbling over mountains
Blues
      turning grey over you
Owls
      hooting rooks cawing
Wind
      rushing thrushes singing
Water
      splashing over stones in an empty
Valley
      green with wild garlic.

5

"Gathering woodland lilies
Myriads blow together" – Tennyson, *"Maud" XII, ii.*

April/time to remember the death of January poets
April/rocks cropping through grass like teeth
April/and I'm blasting your name into limestone on distant
   hillsides
April/dogs brindled like cows running down country lanes
April/girls making the night air hideous with their thighs

April/in bluejeans plump like sardines
April/sermons in stones and malteserpackets in hedges
April/violets and woodanemones amongst the trees to send
    you in letters

6

mornintide and eventide
eventide and mornintide
Death you is ma woman now
You
        is
            ma
                woman
                    now.

Welcome to my World

"Don't find me"
snarl the poems
from the headlines
    "Ne me trouvez
pas" cry
the objects
from the beaches.

Adrian Henri's Talking After Christmas Blues

Well I woke up this mornin' it was Christmas Day
And the birds were singing the night away
I saw my stocking lying on the chair
Looked right to the bottom but you weren't there
there was
          apples
            oranges
              chocolates
                . . . aftershave
– but no you.

So I went downstairs and the dinner was fine
There was pudding and turkey and lots of wine
And I pulled those crackers with a laughing face
Till I saw there was no one in your place
there was
          mincepies
           brandy
            nuts and raisins   ·
              . . . mashed potato
– but no you.

Now it's New Year and it's Auld Lang Syne
And it's 12 o'clock and I'm feeling fine
Should Auld Acquaintance be Forgot?
I don't know girl, but it hurts a lot
there was
          whisky
          vodka
            dry Martini (stirred
              but not shaken)
. . . and 12 New Year resolutions
– all of them about you.

So it's all the best for the year ahead
As I stagger upstairs and into bed
Then I looked at the pillow by my side
. . . I tell you baby I almost cried
there'll be
        Autumn
          Summer
            Spring
                . . . and Winter
– all of them without you.

Four Seasons Poems

SPRING POEM

Spring doing 100
down the motorway of winter

SUMMER POEM

(*for the Shangri-Las*)

Remember
(walkin' in the sand)

AUTUMN POEM

Her
    tears
        fell

Like autumn

WINTER POEM

When I'm with you
I'm as happy as the day is short.

See the Conkering Heroine Comes

Thinking about you
Walking the woods in Autumn
jumping for branches picking glossy horse-chestnuts from the
    ground
caught purple-handed coming back from blackberrying
Walking handinhand in the summer park
flowers dropping on you as we walk through the palmhouse.
magenta to pink to faded rose
pink hearts floating on tiny waterfalls
the woods echoing to the song of the Mersey Bowmen
leaves you said were the colour of the green sweets in
    Mackintosh's Weekend
cheeks warm and smooth like peaches not apples
hair caught golden in the sunlight
your child's eyes wondering at the colour of rhododendrons
and the whiteness of swans.

Coming back in Autumn
the air loud with the colours of Saturdayafternoon football
the alleyway of trees they planted for us in summer
still there
young appletrees going to sleep in their applepie beds
tropical plants in the palmhouse you said
looked like lions sticking their tongues out
one faded pink flower left
leaves falling very slowly in the tropical afternoon inside
you suddenly seeing a family of mice
living high up in the painted wroughtiron girders.

Walking back
the lakes cold the rhododendrons shivering slightly in the
    dusk
peacocks closing up their tails till next summer
your hand in mine
the first frost of winter touching your cheeks.

Winterpoem

(for Elizabeth)

See the conquering hero winter comes
Frost on the palmhouse windows mist covering the
    flowerbeds
Swans somehow not frozen into their lakes
Taking our walk instead in the city
Out of the warm
Neat   O'Cedar floor you just polished

Snow up steps corrugated-iron door black wall
Cathedral disappeared into the mist
Only the railings hard fringed with white like the
    laurel-leaves
Tiny drops of water frozen before falling
Snow stained pink with ash round doorstep and dustbins
Railings
Pagoda in the square Japanese with willow trees for us
Violet cellophane sweet paper singing against pavement
    snow
Cold hands through woolly gloves

Writing this in summer wondering
Where are the snows of yesterday?

Travel Songs

Songs of a Wayfarer for Deirdre

1

Rose   Bay
Willow   Herb
reminds me of you
but
men working in triangular allotments
alongside railway bridges
full of runnerbean sticks
and a fire lighted
at the
apex
remind me of my childhood
like the landscape rushing past
elderflowers   dusty grass   moorhens on quiet ponds
small rivers rushing under trees

2

Poppies are the opiate of the landscape

shocking pink roses in
quiet suburban gardens.

3

"Who liveth alone longeth for mercy.
Makers mercy. Though he must traverse
tracts of sea, sick at heart . . ."
                _ "The Wanderer'
Thinking of you
Where shorelights make bright
The darkling river where
Ignorant ferries pass by night

Cheshire looked marvellous tonight
The train taking me towards you and the sun
Reflected in the banks of green canals
Sitting
Reading of Proud Agamemnon
His armour burnished as the rails
Stretched ahead in the sunlight
Green wasteland suddenly dazzling with purple lupins
Turner standing on the riverbank painting the sunset behind
    factories
Seen through the crisscross dazzle of bridges.

5

Hull Poem

Green phoneboxes for a colourblind population
Brown dogs driving Morris Minors down Anlaby Street
White rabbit against bright green grass
dark rabbitears sticking up against green horizon

Beautiful girls who
can't tell stalks from buttercups
A daisychain pressed in the book this poem's written in
White pebbles under our feet on beaches
where the North Sea is spurned by the headlands
Waves of Debussy breaking over the girls making curry in the
    kitchen
People lying like fishingboats alongside settees after parties

Kissing under a streetlamp
then
Walking back down the dark street with no ending.

6

Railways traverse
Flowers make bright
The secret gardens of our night

7

Scotland 1966

Scotland/finding newlycaught fish lying on the cobblestones
        in mysterious quayside darkness
Scotland/flowers brighter in morning gardens
Scotland/coffee and morning rolls
Scotland/people playing their morning rôles
Scotland/my friends not being dismissed by the Leith police
Scotland/ring round the moon over Georgian terrace houses
Scotland/office girls eating sandwiches off Covenanters'
        graves
Scotland/a piper playing wild laments for the dying land-
        scapes in theatre lounges
Scotland/Alan Breck Stewart dodging from rock to rock in the
        floodlit shadows
Scotland/LIVERPOOL POET INDECENTLY ASSAULTED BY GIRL FOLK-
        SINGER IN THE GRASSMARKET, COURT TOLD
Scotland/meeting someone I'd always wanted to meet at a
        party and not knowing how it felt
Scotland/dream schoolgirl refusing curry in an allnight café
Scotland/Rangers supporters sailing down the Clyde in an
        orange submarine
Scotland/postmen singing songs for love and whisky in
        public houses
Scotland/a bronze dog waiting patiently for its master outside
        a public house
Scotland/John Knox behind the counter shouting 'Time
        Please' at Sandy Bell's
Scotland/the beer tastes even better this year
Scotland/I don't seem to be tasting anything else

Scotland/the fish are even bigger in the chipshops this year
Scotland/hollyhocks and hydrangeas heavy in the afternoon
        sunlight
Scotland/bright pink petals on deep green lawns
Scotland/seeing my childhood in museumcases cigarette-
        cards sweet coupons Hotspur Rover The Beano
        Aeroplane Kits toy soldiers
Scotland/seeing my childhood in conversation lozenges
        saying I LOVE YOU in shopwindows
Scotland/wanting to build a monument to you on Calton Hill
Scotland/wind shaking the appletrees in the garden sitting
        reading a letter from you
Scotland/trees hills sunlight letters poems flowers postcards
        for you pipers singers fishingboats echoing through
        granite streets and empty landscapes.

Nightsong

So we'll go no more a-raving
So late into the night
Though the heart be still as loving
And the neonsigns so bright

Ate my breakfast egg this morning
playing records from last night
woke to hear the front door closing
as the sky was getting light

No more fish-and-chips on corners
Watching traffic going by
No more branches under streetlamps
No more leaves against the sky

No more blues by Otis Redding
No more coffee no more bread
No more dufflecoats for bedding
No more cushions for your head

Though the night is daylight-saving
And the day returns too soon
Still we'll go no more a-raving
By the light of the moon

I Want to Paint

Part One

I want to paint
2000 dead birds crucified on a background of night
Thoughts that lie too deep for tears
Thoughts that lie too deep for queers
Thoughts that move at 186,000 miles/second
The Entry of Christ into Liverpool in 1966
The Installation of Roger McGough to the Chair of Poetry at
    Oxford
Francis Bacon making the President's Speech at the Royal
    Academy Dinner

I want to paint
50 life-sized nudes of Marianne Faithfull
(all of them painted from life)
Welsh Maids by Welsh Waterfalls
Heather Holden as Our Lady of Haslingden
A painting as big as Piccadilly full of neon signs buses
Christmas decorations and beautiful girls with dark blonde
    hair shading their faces

I want to paint
The assassination of the entire Royal Family
Enormous pictures of every pavingstone in Canning Street
The Beatles composing a new National Anthem
Brian Patten writing poems with a flamethrower on disused
    ferryboats
A new cathedral 50 miles high made entirely of pramwheels
An empty Woodbine packet covered in kisses
I want to paint
A picture made from the tears of dirty-faced children in
    Chatham Street

I want to paint
I LOVE YOU across the steps of St George's Hall
I want to paint
                pictures.

Part Two

I want to paint
The Simultaneous and Historical Faces of Death
10,000 shocking pink hearts with your name on
The phantom negro postmen who bring me money in my
    dreams
The first plastic daffodil of spring pushing its way
through the OMO packets in the Supermarket
The portrait of every 6th-form schoolgirl in the country
A full-scale map of the world with YOU at the centre
An enormous lily-of-the-valley with every flower on a
    separate canvas

Lifesize jellybabies shaped like Hayley Mills
A black-and-red flag flying over Parliament
I want to paint
Every car crash on all the motorways of England
Père Ubu drunk at 11 o'clock at night in Lime Street
A SYSTEMATIC DERANGEMENT OF ALL THE SENSES
in black running letters 50 miles high over Liverpool

I want to paint
Pictures that children can play hopscotch on
Pictures that can be used as evidence at murder trials
Pictures that can be used to advertise cornflakes
Pictures that can be used to frighten naughty children
Pictures worth their weight in money
Pictures that tramps can live in
Pictures that children would find in their stockings on
	Christmas morning
Pictures that teenage lovers can send each other
I want to paint
			pictures.

Lakeland Poems

(for Kurt Schwitters, William Wordsworth, and Fiona Stirling Macfarlane)

1

The landscape is full of other people's paintings!

2

The roar of tourist traffic is so loud William Wordsworth is turning in his grave whether he wants to or not.

3

We came to lakeland lonely, empty-handed
and were greeted with
no parking
no camping.
lighting fires forbidden.
Not suitable for
Motor vehicles

4

LAKELAND TERRORISTS COMMIT FURTHER OUTRAGES
Motorists pelted with bluebells

5

I wanted to put a polythene daffodil on Wordsworth's
grave but didn't know where it was, anyway.

6

LIVERPOOL DADAISTS IN BAN-THE-DAFFODIL MARCHES!

7

At length came we to the Chapel Perilous/but
the King was dead/Empty barn smelling of
damp/a pile of dusty 78's/camera eaten by
rust/an unfinished landscape twisted and buckled/
And the wall, half-finished./We said Goodbye
to the old man with plusfours and his dog
& cat & 6 hens & 3 geese/and his memories.

8

Toads. She said. Toads.
The toads roared past ignoring her unpraised thumb
White shorts/cornflake-blue shirt/thighs pink
and slightly mottled like a baby's

9

She held a blue flower against the blue sky. Look
she said. Later we saw a blue car against a
blue tent in a field full of bluebells.

26

Scotland

Part One: The Journey

I keep seeing your name in the blue-and-white lettering every halfmile along the motorway.

Lakeland: where Fiona lives on the other side of glittering water seen through the trees.
Lakeland: where the landscape is too true to be good
Lakeland: where Heather works gathering eggs from still-warm nests in the soft lakeland morning.
Lakeland: where we took the wrong turning.
Lakeland: where the water is cold and clear and grey and looks so cold it would make your teeth hurt.

Cheviots and Teviots: hills that look like watercolours on the landings of furnished flats.

little towns along the road where the entire population turn out on Sunday afternoons to watch the trafficlights change/ heather is always on distant hills/or tied up in ribbons and too expensive to buy.

Part Two: Edinburgh

In Scotland

        Fish and chips is called Fish Supper

In Scotland

        There don't seem to be any pretty girls

In Scotland

        Vinegar is white not brown

In Scotland

        All buildings look like very beautiful prisons

In Scotland

        Bitter is called Heavy

In Scotland
                    Black Puddings are sometimes White
In Scotland
                    Cornish Pasties are called Bridies
In Scotland
                    Poems come tartan giftwrapped

Floodlit ghosts parade the castle walls
And phantom redcoats hunt their kilted prey down Princes St.

A conversation:
"All Germans seem terribly cold"
"Yes, they are, rather"
"It's a wonder they ever produced any writers"
*"Maybe there are a few warm ones and the cold ones drove them
into becoming poets"*

Edvard Munch looking out of a shrubbery in the Botanical
Gardens
Watching the young lovers on sunlit benches

Part Three: Nightride and Sunrise

WAV 2515
1.30 Ed. – 7.22 Liv. 30/7d.
St Andrews Sq. Plat. A.

One lonely tree on a Scottish hillside
Against a sky by Delacroix
Me in the foreground awake
In a coachload of sleeping people

Outriders of mist pacing our headlights
Thinning to peachbloom on moonlit fields

THERE ARE NO CAFES IN CARLISLE

Walls now make hearts on a stick
Instant love with chocolate covering
Icecream and raspberry on the inside
And you in the middle

SHAP FELL THIS MORNIN'

Keswick where we took the wrong turning coming

We came down out of the hills and
suddenly the sea like a change of scenery/dawn came
striped green and yellow along the motorway

flat red sun
mist
    creeping along green canals
passing
the allotments where I used to paint
and the corner where I used to meet Joyce at dinnertime

"LIVERPOOL: ALL OFF PLEASE"

People fumble for luggage like a poet
fumbling for words
and out into the city morning
like a poet with nothing to say.

Liverpool Poems

1

GO TO WORK ON A BRAQUE!

2

Youths disguised as stockbrokers
Sitting on the grass eating the Sacred Mushroom.

3

Liverpool I love your horny-handed tons of soil.

4

PRAYER FROM A PAINTER TO ALL CAPITALISTS:

Open your wallets and repeat after me
"HELP YOURSELF!"

5

There's one way of being sure of keeping fresh
LIFEBUOY helps you rise again on the 3rd day
after smelling something that smelt like other people's socks.

6

Note for a definition of optimism:
A man trying the door of Yates Wine Lodge
At quarter past four in the afternoon.

7

I have seen Père UBU walking across Lime St
And Alfred Jarry cycling down Elliott Street.

30

8

And I saw DEATH in Upper Duke St
Cloak flapping black tall Batman collar
Striding tall shoulders down the hill past the Cathedral
    brown shoes slightly down at the heel.

9

Unfrocked Chinese mandarins holding lonely feasts in
Falkner Sq gardens to enjoy the snow

10

Prostitutes in the snow in Canning St like strange erotic
    snowmen
And Marcel Proust in the Kardomah eating Madeleine butties
    dipped in tea.

11

Wyatt James Virgil and Morgan Earp with Doc Holliday
Shooting it out with the Liver Birds at the Pier Head.

12

And a Polish gunman young beautiful dark glasses
combatjacket/staggers down Little St Bride St blood
dripping moaning clutches/collapses down a back jigger
coughing/falls in a wilderness of Dazwhite washing.

Meat Poem

You skewer through me
bleeding electric
on the brightlylit supermarket counters
of your mind

Salad Poem

(for Henri Rousseau le Douanier)

The sun is shining outside
Henri Rousseau (Gentil Rousseau)
The sky is blue
   like your skies
I want to paint the salad
on the table
bright crisp green red purple
lettuce and radishes, ham and tomatoes
Paint them like your jungles
Gentle Rousseau
I want to paint
   All things bright and beautiful
   All salads great and small
I want to make
   Blue skies bluer
   Green grass greener
   Pink flowers brighter
     Like you
        Henri Rousseau.

32

The Fairy Feller's Master-Stroke

(for Richard Dadd, Maurice Cockrill and Susan Rainbow)

You climb up the Nutwood hills
your check scarf and woolly gloves
sitting watching the rocks alive with snowdrops
the cracks in the limestone
when you go for tea
filling with fairy folk
long noses some faces broader than long
swarming round your drawing board
muscles straining to lift paint-tubes
"a vague people
living beneath the roots
of trees"
carve
the leaden daisies
lift
the heavy axe
killing the old king
glossy chestnuts
rolling
over painted rocks.

Bomb Commercials

(for two voices)

1 A. Get PAD nuclear meat for humans
   B. Don't give your family ordinary meat, give them PAD
   A. P.A.D. – Prolongs Active Death
   B. Enriched with nourishing marrowbone strontium.

2 A. All over the world, more and more people are changing
      to
                          BOMB
   B. BOMB – The international passport to smoking ruins

3 B. . . . . *so then I said "well let's all go for a picnic and we went
      and it was all right except for a bit of sand in the butties and
      then of course the wasps and Michael fell in the river but
      what I say is you can't have everything perfect can you so
      just then there was a big bang and the whole place caught fire
      and something happened to Michael's arm and I don't know
      what happened to my Hubby and its perhaps as well as there
      were only four pieces of Kit-Kat so we had one each and then
      we had to walk home 'cos there weren't any buses. . . ."*
   A. HAVE A BREAK – HAVE A KIT-KAT

4 A. Everyday in cities all over England people are breathing
      in Fall-out
   B. Get the taste of the Bomb out of your mouth with OVAL
      FRUITS

5 A. General Howard J. Sherman has just pressed the button
      that killed 200 million people. A BIG job with BIG respon-
      sibilities. The General has to decide between peace and
      the extinction of the human race. . . .
   B. But he can't tell Stork from Butter.

Short Stories

1   I can't communicate with you because the postmen are on strike. Who do I blame when we're together?

2   "There's this bird man who works in this shop in Liverpool." I think about him/sun melting the wax on his feathers/plunging headlong into the Mersey.

3   I ran my fingers up her bare arm up to her throat. Should I do it now? Now or never. There's someone watching! The moon watches cold and white through the gap in the curtains.

4   Sunlight. Gardens. Children playing. Icecream van playing. Greyhouses through the railings. Black faces white faces brown faces. She turns, smiling. . . .

5   Afterwards they walked back together hand-in-hand. "Wouldn't it be funny if it happened now," he said. She looked up. The bloodred fireball blotted out the sky.

6   I couldn't move. I could hear the hiss and crunch of the tyres. I could feel the engine's hot breath, smell the stink of petrol. "Its best friend should tell it," I thought as everything went black. . . .

Summer Poems Without Words

(To be distributed in leaflet form to the audience. Each poem should be tried within the next seven days.)

1   Try to imagine your next hangover.

2   ·Travel on the Woodside ferry with your eyes closed. Travel back with them open.

3   Look for a black cat. Stroke it. This will be either lucky or unlucky.

4   Find a plastic flower. Hold it up to the light.

5   Next time you see someone mowing a lawn smell the smell of freshly cut grass.

6   Watch *Coronation Street*. Listen to the "B" side of the latest Dusty Springfield record.

7   Sit in a city square in the sunlight. Remember the first time you made love.

8   Look at every poster you pass next time you're on a bus.

9   Open the *News of the World* at page 3. Read between the lines.

10 The next time you clean your teeth *think* about what you're doing.

The New "Our Times"

(for Felix Fénéon)

1

At 3 p.m. yesterday, a Mr Adolphus Edwards, a Jamaican immigrant, was pecked to death by a large Bronze Eagle in Upper Parliament St. A US State Dept spokesman said later, "We have no comment to make as of this time."

2

Police-Constable George Williams, who was partially blinded by a 15lb jellybaby thrown at a passing pop singer, is to be retired on half-pension.

3

Bearded Liverpool couple put out of misery in night by drip oil heater, court told.

4

A certain Mrs Elspeth Clout, of Huyton, was killed by an unidentified falling object. It was thought to be a particularly hard stool evacuated from the toilet of a passing aeroplane.

5

2 chip-shop proprietors were today accused of selling human ears fried in batter. One of them said: "We believe there is room for innovation in the trade."

6

Fatality in Kardomah bomb outrage: Waitress buried Alive under two thousand Danish pastries.

7

At the inquest on Paul McCartney, aged 21, described as a popular singer and guitarist, P.C. Smith said, in evidence, that he saw one of the accused, Miss Jones, standing waving bloodstained hands shouting "I got a bit of his liver".

Batpoem

(*for Bob Kane and The Almost Blues*)

Take me back to Gotham City
        Batman
Take me where the girls are pretty
        Batman
All those damsels in distress
Half-undressed or even less
The BatPill makes 'em all say Yes
        Batman

Help us out in Vietnam
        Batman
Help us drop that BatNapalm
        Batman
Help us bomb those jungle towns
Spreading pain and death around
Coke 'n' Candy wins them round
        Batman

Help us smash the Vietcong
        Batman
Help us show them that they're wrong
        Batman
Help us spread democracy
Get them high on LSD
Make them just like you and me
        Batman

Show me what I have to do
        Batman
'Cause I want to be like you
        Batman
Flash your Batsign over Lime Street
Batmobiles down every crimestreet
Happy Batday that's when I'll meet
        Batman

38

3

Dear
We ho   .e are pl
commences o.   ∠OWIE !!
5/- postal order plus 6d postage and packing for membersh
Remember, the Fan Club commences September 1st. Jo

Universes

(for Edward Lucie-Smith)

2 Poems for H.P. Lovecraft

1

Miskatonic river
Flowing through a landscape that is always evening
Accusing eyes
in the empty streets of Innsmouth
Strange movements out on the reef
Tumuli on hilltops
Trembling in the thunder
Behind the gambrel roofs of Arkham.

2

"Ph'nglui mgw'nafh Cthulhu R'lyeh wgah'nagl fhtagn"

"In his house at R'lyeh
Great Cthulhu sleeps"

amid
alien geometries
perspectives
walls shifting as you watch them
slumbering
in the Cyclopean dripping gloom
waiting to wake like Leviathan
when his children shall call him.

Four Lovepoems for Ray Bradbury

1

sitting
holding your eight hands
on the bank of the dry red canal

2   *(for Mike Evans)*

you toss your long hair
and look at me with witcheyes

you kiss me
and disappear

my heart bursting
like an April balloon.

3

*"And I'll always remember
the first time we went out together"*
Your eyes misty behind the glass
Earthlight shining in your hair

4

the day before the Carnival leaves town.

a shy dwarf
waiting by the boardwalk
for the beautiful dancer
who never comes

Poem for Gully Foyle

*"Gully Foyle is my name
Terra is my nation
Deep space is my dwelling place
And Death's my destination"*

Gouffre Martel. Darkness.
Under the rock and earth a voice
Lying your tigerface blazing in the dark
Listening to her
Your mind still trapped in the broken spaceship

Flaming man appearing like your vengeance
On the beach, in the 3-ring cosmic circus
Your scarred body your tattooed face
Leaping between Aldebaran and Ceres
Eternity at your feet. The stars your destination.

Galactic Lovepoem

(*for Susan*)

Warm your feet at the sunset
Before we go to bed
Read your book by the light of Orion
With Sirius guarding your head
Then reach out and switch off the planets
We'll watch them go out one by one
You kiss me and tell me you love me
By the light of the last setting sun
We'll both be up early tomorrow
A new universe has begun.

Car Crash Blues *or* Old Adrian Henri's Interminable Talking Surrealistic Blues

(for Jim Dine and Ch. Baudelaire)

You make me feel like
someone's driven me into a wall
baby
You make me feel like
Sunday night at the village hall
baby
You make me feel like a Desert Rat
You make me feel like a Postman's hat
You make me feel like I've been swept under the mat
baby

You make me feel like
something from beyond the grave
baby
You make me feel like
Woolworth's After-Shave
baby
You make me feel like a drunken nun
You make me feel like the war's begun
You make me feel like I'm being underdone
baby

You make me feel like
a Wellington filled with blood
baby
You make me feel like
my clothes are made of wood
baby
You make me feel like a Green Shield stamp
You make me feel like an army camp
You make me feel like a bad attack of cramp
baby

You make me feel like
a limestone quarry
baby
You make me feel like
a Corporation lorry
baby
You make me feel like a hideous sore
You make me feel like a hardware store
You make me feel like something spilt on the floor
baby

You make me feel like
a used Elastoplast
baby
You make me feel like
a broken plastercast
baby
You make me feel like an empty lift
You make me feel like a worthless gift
You make me feel like a slagheap shifting
baby

You make me feel like
last week's knickers
baby
You make me feel like
2 consenting vicars
baby
You make me feel like an overgrown garden
You make me feel like a traffic warden
You make me feel like General Gordon
baby
like a hunchback's hump
like a petrol pump
like the girl
    on the ledge
        that's afraid to jump

like a
    a garbage truck
        with a heavy load on
        baby

Adrian Henri's Last Will and Testament

"No one owns life, but anyone who can pick up a frying pan owns death."

William Burroughs

To whom it may concern:

As my imminent death is hourly expected these days/
car brakes screaming on East Lancs tarmac/trapped
in the blazing cinema/mutely screaming I TOLD YOU SO
from melting eyeballs as the whitehot fireball
dissolves the Cathedral/being the first human being to die
of a hangover/dying of over-emotion after seeing 20
schoolgirls waiting at a zebracrossing.

I appoint Messrs Bakunin and Kropotkin my executors and
make the following provisions:

1   I leave my priceless collections of Victorian Oil Lamps,
photographs of Hayley Mills, brass fenders and Charlie
Mingus records to all Liverpool poets under 23 who are
also blues singers and failed sociology students.

2   I leave the entire East Lancs Road with all its landscapes to
the British people.

45

3   I hereby appoint Wm. Burroughs my literary executor, instructing him to cut up my collected works and distribute them through the public lavatories of the world.

4   Proceeds from the sale of relics: locks of hair, pieces of floorboards I have stood on, fragments of bone flesh teeth bits of old underwear etc. to be given to my widow.

5   I leave my paintings to the Nation with the stipulation that they must be exhibited in Public Houses, Chip Shops, Coffee Bars and Cellar Clubs throughout the country.

6   Proceeds from the sale of my other effects to be divided equally amongst the 20 most beautiful schoolgirls in England (these to be chosen after due deliberation and exhaustive tests by an informal committee of my friends).

Witnessed this day by: Adrian Henri
James Ensor   Jan. '64
Charlie "Bird" Parker

Love Is . . .

Love is feeling cold in the back of vans
Love is a fanclub with only two fans
Love is walking holding paintstained hands
Love is

Love is fish and chips on winter nights
Love is blankets full of strange delights
Love is when you don't put out the light
Love is

Love is the presents in Christmas shops
Love is when you're feeling Top of the Pops
Love is what happens when the music stops
Love is

Love is white panties lying all forlorn
Love is a pink nightdress still slightly warm
Love is when you have to leave at dawn
Love is

Love is you and love is me
Love is a prison and love is free
Love's what's there when you're away from me
Love is . . .

Who?

Who can I
spend my life
with
Who can I
listen to Georges Brassens
singing
"Les amoureux des bancs publiques"
with
Who can I
go to Paris with
getting drunk at night with
tall welldressed spades
Who can I
quarrel with
outside chipshops
in sidestreets
on landings
Who else
can sing along with Shostakovitch
Who else
would sign a Christmas card
"Cannonball"
Who else
can work the bathroom geyser
Who else
drinks as much bitter
Who else
makes all my favourite meals
except the ones I make
myself
Who else
would bark back at dogs
in the moonlit lamplight streets
Who else
would I find
waiting dark bigeyed

in a corner of a provincial jazzclub
You say
we don't get on
anymore
but
who can I
laugh on beaches with
wondering at the noise
the limpets make
still sucking in the tide
Who
can I
buy
my next Miles Davis record
to share with
who
makes coffee the way I like it
and
love the way I used to like it
who
came in from the sun
the day
the world went spinning away
from me
who
doesn't wash the clothes I always want
who
spends my money
who
wears my dressing gown
and always leaves the sleeves turned up
who
makes me feel
as empty as the house does
when she's not there
who
else
but
you

For Joyce

Love From Arthur Rainbow

In a villa called "Much Bickering"
In a street called Pleasant Street
Living with her wicked parents
Was a princess, small and neat

She wanted to be an artist
So off to a college she went
And as long as she got a Diploma
They considered it money well spent

One day she met a poet
Who taught her all about life
He walked her down to the station
Then went back home to his wife

He came from the end of the rainbow
At least that's what she thought
The kind of love she wanted
The kind that can't be bought

But time and the last train to the suburbs
Killed the love that would never die
And he'll find another love
And she'll sit at home and cry

Now she's reading through his letters
In her small schoolteacher flat
Dusty paint-tubes in the corner
Worn-out "Welcome" on the mat

O the day she met Arthur Rainbow
There were roses all over town
There were angels in all the shopwindows
And kisses not rain coming down

Now it's off to work every morning
And back home for dinner at eight
For the gold at the end of the rainbow
Lies buried beneath her front gate.

Morning Poem

(*for Deirdre*)

"I've just about reached
breaking point"
he snapped.

Love Story

You keep our love hidden
like the nightdress you keep under your pillow
and never wear when I'm there

But
one sunfilled day
you took me to your magic room
at the end of the yellow corridor
and showed me enchanted stilllifes
Nivea tins Bodymist sprays cold cream jars
glowing like jewels
your body singing pink in the sunlight
opening to me like the red pulsing heart of a flower
in Public Gardens
where peacocks open their thousand eyes for us
and birdpeople move noiselessly
through the dripping palmhouse
feeling your body under me
warm and alive as the grass under our feet

I LOVE YOU

When listening to Bruckner in the sunlit bathroom
When the hills and valleys of your morning body
are hidden from my gaze by Body Mist
When I don't have to ask who it is on the telephone
When we can't wait till the programme finishes
When I slip out quietly leaving you to sleep
untroubled dreams till morning in your darkened room
When I walk out into the dark shining streets
bright signs from petrolstations lamplight on leaves
hard unyielding lights from city flats

I LOVE YOU

Walking home yellow moon over the rooftops
cars crawling girls stopping everywhere smelling of you
Going off to sleep still smelling the rich luxury lather in
                                          your hair
Walking holding your mini-hand
Standing in the Saturdaymorning bank
hot with people worrying about money
Seeing half a bottle of gin smashed on the pavement
Even when seeing schoolgirls on buses
their blackstockinged knees in mourning for their lost
virginity

I LOVE YOU

on trains
in cars
on buses
in taxis

I LOVE YOU

in that midnight hour
when all the clocks stopped
and it was midsummer
for ever

Mrs Albion, You've Got a Lovely Daughter

(for Allen Ginsberg)

Albion's most lovely daughter sat on the banks of the Mersey
    dangling her landing stage in the water.

The daughters of Albion
    arriving by underground at Central Station
    eating hot ecclescakes at the Pierhead
    writing "Billy Blake is fab" on a wall in Mathew St

    taking off their navyblue schooldrawers and
    putting on nylon panties ready for the night

The daughters of Albion
    see the moonlight beating down on them in Bebington
    throw away their chewinggum ready for the goodnight kiss
sleep in the dinnertime sunlight with old men
    looking up their skirts in St Johns Gardens
comb their darkblonde hair in suburban bedrooms
powder their delicate little nipples/wondering if tonight will
    be the night
their bodies pressed into dresses or sweaters
lavender at The Cavern or pink at The Sink

The daughters of Albion wondering how to explain why they
    didn't go home

The daughters of Albion
    taking the dawn ferry to tomorrow
    worrying about what happened
    worrying about what hasn't happened
    lacing up blue sneakers over brown ankles
    fastening up brown stockings to blue supenderbelts

Beautiful boys with bright red guitars
in the spaces between the stars

Reelin' an' a-rockin'
Wishin' an' a-hopin'
Kissin' an' a-prayin'
Lovin' an' a-layin'

Mrs Albion, you've got a lovely daughter.

In the Midnight Hour

When we meet
in the midnight hour
country girl
I will bring you nightflowers
coloured like your eyes
in the moonlight
in the midnight
hour

I remember

Your cold hand
held for a moment among strangers
held for a moment among dripping trees
in the midnight hour

I remember

Your eyes coloured like the autumn landscape
walking down muddy lanes
watching sheep eating yellow roses
walking in city squares in winter rain
kissing in darkened hallways

walking in empty suburban streets
saying goodnight in deserted alleyways

in the midnight hour

Andy Williams singing "We'll keep a Welcome in the Hill-
    sides" for us
When I meet you at the station
The Beatles singing "We can Work it Out" with James Ensor at
    the harmonium
Rita Hayworth in a nightclub singing "Amade Mia"
I will send you armadas
of love vast argosies of flowers
in the midnight hour
country girl

when we meet

in the
moonlight
midnight
hour
country girl

I will bring you

yellow
white
eyes
bright
moon
light
mid
night
flowers
in the midnight hour.

Don't Worry/Everything's Going to Be All Right

Don't worry
If your boyfriend doesn't treat you right
baby
Everything's going to be all right
come with me
And every poem I write will have your name in it
Don't worry
If the factories and villas cover the countryside
Everything's going to be all right
England will be given back to the animals
and we'll find a home under fernleaves known only to foxes
Don't worry
If I can't afford to buy you coffee after school
Everything's going to be all right
Soon the poem will replace the pound sterling as international
    currency
and Britain will get on the poem standard again
Don't worry
About those lunatics in the government
Everything's going to be all right
The country will be governed by beautiful girls under 18
(and you will let me carry your portfolio home from the
    House)
Don't worry
About what happened the other night
Everything's going to be all right
They'll give you contraceptive pills shaped
    like jellybabies with your milk at playtime
Don't worry
about what your Dad says about the younger generation
Everything's going to be all right
There'll be involuntary euthanasia for everyone over 30
not a poet painter or musician
Don't worry

About the rain
Everything's going to be all right
The streets will be covered with tiny pink flowers
like the ones on your suspenderbelt
Bathingsuits will be banned from beaches
School uniforms will be the only kind allowed in public
Your end-of-term report will be marked out of 100 for sex
  appeal
(and you will be Top of the Form)
Policemen will be beaten up by poets
Trade Unions will be taken over by workers
There'll be 24-hour licensing
And everything will be on the National Drink Service
your parents will wake us every morning with breakfast
Your teacher will smile at notes saying we stayed in bed late
Your face will be in every art gallery
Your name in every book of poetry
So
Don't worry
Everything's going to be all right.

Remember

And somewhere
it will always be Whitsun and summer
with sandals to keep the rain from your sunburnt feet
And you will have just given me a bunch of artificial flowers
lilies-of-the-valley made of cloth with stiff glossy leaves
And turn and wave goodbye smiling
hair over your eyes caught in sunlight by the windowframe
. . . Remember?

Liverpool 8

Liverpool 8. . . . A district of beautiful, fading, decaying Georgian terrace houses. . . . Doric columns supporting peeling entablatures, dirty windows out of Vitruvius concealing families of happy Jamaicans, sullen out-of-work Irishmen, poets, queers, thieves, painters, university students, lovers. . . .

The streets named after Victorian elder statesmen like Huskisson, the first martyr to the age of communications whose choragic monument stands in the tumble-down graveyard under the cathedral. . . . The cathedral which dominates our lives, pink at dawn and grey at sunset. . . . The cathedral towering over the houses my friends live in. . . .

Beautiful reddish purplish brick walls, pavements with cracked flags where children play hopscotch, the numbers ascending in silent sequence in the mist next morning. . . . Streets where you play out after tea. . . . Back doors and walls with names, hearts, kisses scrawled or painted. . . .

White horses crashing through supermarket windows full of detergent packets. . . . Little girls playing kiss-chase with Mick Jagger in the afternoon streets. . . .

A new cathedral at the end of Hope Street, ex-government surplus from Cape Kennedy ready to blast off taking a million Catholics to a heaven free from Orangemen. . . . Wind blowing inland from Pierhead bringing the smell of breweries and engine oil from ferry boats. . . .

Père Ubu in Liverpool

A Fragment

Time and Place:
Liverpool now

Dramatis Personae:
Père Ubu
Mère Ubu
Palotins
Liverpool bird
Mods
Man in bowler hat

SCENE ONE
(Père Ubu is discovered walking round the corner of Lewis's.)

Ubu (mopping brow):
By my green candle, we are excessively fatigued. (Sees bird standing underneath statue.) Young lady, having recently disembarked from that which crosses the water of the Mersey, we are taking our Royal Person to your splendid Cathedral, which will serve as our Phynancial Quarters, being of suitable magnificence . . .

Bird (aside):
State of 'im!

Ubu:
. . . could you therefore direct the here-present Master of Phynances to the building we have named?

Bird:
Yerwhar?

Ubu:
Hornsgidouille, I cannot communicate with her. I shall try once more. . . .
Mademoiselle?

59

Bird:
Ooer!

Ubu:
Shittr! WHERE ARE WE?

Bird (comprehending):
Oh! Lewis's.

Ubu:
Ah. And that is no doubt a statue of Mr Lewis?

Bird (pointing upward and giggling):
What – *dar*? No. Dat's "Scouse".

Ubu:
And who is that?

Bird:
It's a statue of a feller with no clothes on and, er, all the fellers meet their birds under it and when it's wet the rain drips off 'is thingie and it looks as if he's . . . (dissolves into giggles)

Ubu:
I see. And where are you going, my dunderheaded maid?

Bird:
I'm meetin' me friend Mary and we're goin' to The Cavern.

Ubu:
Ah, yes, I had heard there was a Cavern in the town.

Bird:
I'll 'ave ter go now – tarar!

(She hurries away, watched by Père Ubu. When almost offstage she drops her handbag, shouts "ooer", picks it up again and exits.)

SCENE TWO

(The scene changes to Hardman Street. Père Ubu is discovered toiling up the hill, followed at a distance by Mère Ubu and a number of Palotins.)

Mère Ubu:
Oh, Père Ubu, you big bag of shit, why don't you ask someone the way?

Ubu:
Silence, Mère Ubu, or I'll wring your horrible scrawny neck. (Sees a crowd of Mods leaning against the wall outside The Sink Club. Speaks to the nearest one.) Tell me, sire, could you direct me to that edifice known as the Cathedral?

Mod:
Yerwhar?

Ubu:
Hornsgidouille, shittr, can no one here speak a civilized tongue?

Mod:
Now then, la, yer wanner watch dat languidge yer know.

Ubu (to Mère Ubu and party):
Ignorant savages!

Mod:
Yer lookin' for a spot of lumber, la?

Ubu:
Lumber?

Mod:
You know – a bit of a barney, a punch-up, a KO job like.

62

Ubu:
Do you dare to challenge the mighty Master of Phynances himself to battle? The great Père Ubu, King of Poland, Count of Sandomir, Emperor of Liverpool! By my green candle, shittr, sire, a hideous fate shall be yours. Torsion of the nose and ears, extraction of the eyes. Insertion of the Little Piece of Wood into the Nine Entrances of the Body. . . .

Mod:
All right den. I've got me mates here. (Pushes Ubu.)

Ubu:
Forward, Palotins, let the shittr-hook do noble battle! (The Palotins rush forward waving lavatory brushes and start fighting with the Mods. One Mod falls to the ground. Others have got a Palotin on the ground and are putting the boot in. Père Ubu retires to the rear and shouts encouragement. One of the Mods sees him and rushes towards him.)

Mod 2:
I'll get the big feller.

Ubu:
No no don't hurt me I'm on your side Liverpool for the Cup I Love You Yeah Yeah Yeah Long Live King Billy. (By this time he is cowering behind Mère Ubu's skirts. Mod 2 pushes her aside and seizes him.)

Mod 2:
Yer dirty Prodestant bastard! (Butts him.)

Ubu (on ground):
Ooh, I'm dying. Our Phynancial nose, pride of our magnificent body, is irreparably broken. Help me, Mère Ubu!

Mère Ubu:
Help yourself, you bloody great baby.
(The Mods run off. Palotins help Père Ubu to his feet.)

SCENE THREE

(Outside the Philharmonic Hall. Père Ubu, Mère Ubu and the surviving Palotins trudge along Hope Street. Enter a man in a bowler hat, morning suit, briefcase, rolled umbrella etc.)

Ubu:

Ah! At last a worthy-looking citizen. Obviously a Rentier, a man of substance in this city. Perhaps I shall now get some civilized directions . . . Excuse me, sire, but I and my entourage have walked for many hours and our Royal feet are exceedingly sore. Could you perhaps direct us to that which has heretofore been known as the Cathedral?

Man:

Yerwhar? (Ubu collapses.)

CURTAIN

Love Poem/Colour Supplement

It was our first great war
And after the first successful sortie
Into the nomansgland
between her thighs
We waited anxiously every month
for poppysellers to appear in her streets.

Drinking Song

He became more and more drunk
As the afternoon wore off.

Song for a Beautiful Girl Petrol-Pump Attendant on the Motorway

I wanted your soft verges
But you gave me the hard shoulder.

Poem for Roger McGough

A nun in a Supermarket
Standing in the queue
Wondering what it's like
To buy groceries for two.

Dawn Chorus

If I were a blackbird
I'd whistle and sing
And stay in bed until eleven in the morning.

Saturday

(*for Philip Jones Griffiths*)

I spent Saturday
feeling randy
drinking brandy reading *Candy*
to Brahms's Violin Concerto.

Permissive Poem

"Oh mummy dear" the daughter said
Dropping her silver spoon
"*Please* don't say dirty weekend
We call it our mini-moon."

Love Poem

(*for Sydney Hoddes*)

"I love you" he said
With his tongue in her cheek.

Art Poem

(*for Sandy*)

The Mona Lisa isn't smiling!
Perhaps she got out of the wrong side of the canvas this
    morning.

Buttons

Perhaps you don't love me at all,
but at least you sew buttons on my coat
which is more than my wife does.

Cat Poem

You're black and sleek and beautiful
What a pity your best friend won't tell you
Your breath smells of Kit-E-Kat.

Six Landscapes for Susan

1

You
in the country
looking at horses
picking deadly nightshade
observing lesser celandines

2

Pools by factories applegreen
and bright with rainbows

3

Slow doubledecker bus
moving between
red dead mountain bracken
and thin trees veiling the valley
dotted with farms

4

Walking
round a village corner
turning into a doorway
in a large hoarding
into darkness stone stairs smelling of apples
out
into the early morning the
air dazzling with the cries of seagulls
mountain slopes
reared up at the end of the tiny street

5

Bright green ferns through raingrey sky
round railway tunnels in Yorkshire
pale pink roses picked for you
after pie and chips in late night Oldham cafés

6

Palegreen fields powdered with yellow flowers
two cutout men in white with buckets
carrying a sign across a sunlit field
swollen rivers and shining watermeadows
one lapwing
swans
cows wading up to their ankles
poppies in clumps of grass
on purple gravel by the railway line

The Entry of Christ into Liverpool

City morning. dandelionseeds   blowing from wasteground.
smell of overgrown privethedges. children's voices
in the distance. sounds from the river.
round the corner into Myrtle St. Saturdaymorning shoppers
headscarves. shoppingbaskets. dogs.

then
  down the hill

THE SOUND OF TRUMPETS
cheering and shouting in the distance
children running
icecream vans
flags breaking out over buildings
black and red green and yellow
Union Jacks   Red Ensigns
LONG LIVE SOCIALISM
stretched against the blue sky
over St George's hall

Now the procession

THE MARCHING DRUMS
hideous masked Breughel faces of old ladies in the crowd
yellow masks of girls in curlers and headscarves
smelling of factories
Masks   Masks   Masks
red masks   purple masks   pink masks

crushing surging carrying me along
down the hill past the Philharmonic The Labour Exchange
excited feet crushing the geraniums in St Luke's Gardens
placards   banners   posters
Keep Britain White
End the War in Vietnam
God Bless Our Pope

Billboards hoardings drawings on pavements
words painted on the road
STOP GO HALT
the sounds of pipes and drums down the street
little girls in yellow and orange dresses paper flowers
embroidered banners
Loyal Sons of King William Lodge, Bootle
Masks more Masks crowding in off buses
standing on walls climbing fences

familiar faces among the crowd
faces of my friends the shades of Pierre Bonnard and
Guillaume Apollinaire
Jarry cycling carefully through the crowd. A black cat
picking her way underfoot
posters
signs
gleaming salads
COLMAN'S MUSTARD
J. Ensor, Fabriqueur de Masques
HAIL JESUS, KING OF THE JEWS
straining forward to catch a glimpse through the crowd
red hair   white robe   grey donkey
familiar face
trafficlights zebracrossings
GUIN
GUINN
GUINNESS IS
white bird dying unnoticed in a corner
splattered feathers
blood running merged with the neonsigns
in a puddle
GUINNESS IS GOOD
GUINNESS IS GOOD FOR
Masks   Masks   Masks   Masks   Masks
GUINNESS IS GOOD FOR YOU

brassbands cheering loudspeakers blaring
clatter of police horses

ALL POWER TO THE CONSTITUENT
ASSEMBLY
masks cheering glittering teeth
daffodils trodden underfoot

BUTCHERS OF JERUSALEM
banners cheering drunks stumbling and singing
masks
masks
masks

evening
thin sickle moon
pale blue sky
flecked with bright orange clouds
streamers newspapers discarded paper hats
blown slowly back up the hill by the evening wind
dustmen with big brooms sweeping the gutters
last of the crowds waiting at bus-stops
giggling schoolgirls quiet businessmen
me
walking home
empty chip-papers drifting round my feet.

I Suppose You Think It's Funny

I suppose you think it's funny
when your smile opens me like a tin of Kit-E-Kat
I suppose you think it's funny
when perfumed dancers with sequinned tights
fill my Arabian Nights with Turkish Delights

71

I suppose you think it's funny
when your nightdress falls open revealing last year's election
    posters
I suppose you think it's funny
to post the cat and put out my poems instead
I suppose you think it's funny
to hang a photograph of Eichmann over your bed
signed *"Affectionately yours, Adolf"*
I suppose you think it's funny
when the bath breaks out in limegreen spots before my
    astonished gaze
I suppose you think it's funny
to give away the time we've spent to a door-to-door Ancient of
    days
I suppose you think it's funny
to publish my secret identity in the *Liverpool Echo*
I suppose you think it's funny
to fill my Y-fronts with Red Kryptonite
I suppose you think it's funny
to comb your hair like a lion
and push my breakfast through the bars
I suppose you think it's funny
to fill the next door garden with schoolgirls playing guitars
I suppose you think it's funny
when I cover you with flowers
I suppose you think it's funny
when you take an April shower
I suppose you think it's funny
when you've taken all my money
and the bailiff's in the parlour
eating bread and honey
and you meet me in a thunderstorm
and tell me that it's sunny
I suppose *you* think it's funny.

Love Poem

Snow scattering on the windscreen/blowing
from the drystone moors/I think of you.

*London
Poems*

My central nervous system has gone: my
ganglia aren't even on the AA map. My heart is
single-line traffic, one way only.

On the tube after seeing Rauschenberg
the tube a huge construction where he had
cunningly
got people reflected in the windows and
posters moving past

You and Père Ubu holding hands in Piccadilly
Walking off into the COCA COLA sunset

*Heather
Holden, 16,
Haslingden
Grammar
School
"Haslingden
Moors with
Snow"*

Beautiful/Hair falling over eyes/hands cold
    holding sketchbook/
crowded noisy schoolroom/postercolours/tiny
    blue uniform
frozen at the corner of a field/waiting to meet
    her first lover after school

Hate Poem
"To know know know you
Is to love love love you"
And I don't.

Love Poem
ANY RECORD IN THE TOP 20 ANYTIME IS OUR TUNE

An empty Colgate tube

An almond with ALMOND written on it

breakfastpink gingham shirt & red waistcoat like
   tomatoes

a bar of rock lettered all through with your name

and a plastic flower

a pair of your old navyblue schooldrawers

an empty Drambuie bottle & an empty packet of
   export cigarettes

a signed copy of this poem

a chocolate Easter Egg

A photograph:

Little smiling girl in bra and knickers sitting
in a summer field

A red bra with I LOVE YOU written inside one of
   the cups

A painting of a shocking pink heart with your name
   scratched on it

Some rusting scissors and a decaying fan from a dead
   King's treasurehouse.

Assemblage of Objects and Mementoes

"Bluetit Patrol 2nd 15th Rossendale Girl Guides' Summer Camp Arnside 1960"

Our love is watched over by all my masters;   *Manchester Poem*

Picabia watches from his cacodynamic eye

Max Ernst looks on as impersonally as when he
   watched

the Virgin Mary spanking the infant Jesus

Guillaume Apollinaire in Piccadilly Bus Station

watches the unlikely couple walking the cold streets

Monk takes his hands off the keyboard and smiles
   approvingly

The Beatles sing lullabys for our never-to-happen children

Quietly in the shadows by Central Station

William Burroughs sits dunking Pound Cake in coffee waiting
   for the last connection

and sees us through the window

Bartok has orchestrated the noise of the tulips in Piccadilly
 . Gardens for us

Marcel Duchamp has added your photograph to the Green
    Box
Dylan Thomas staggers into the Cromwell for one last one
and waves across to us
Kurt Schwitters smiles as he picks up the two pink bus tickets
we have just thrown away
Parker blows another chorus of Loverman for us
Ensor smiles behind his mask
Jarry cycles slowly behind us down Spring Gardens

Rauschenberg and Jasper Johns
Bless the bed we lie upon

Daffodils grow in the shadows of your hair   *Lakeland*
Waterfalls in the hollows of your throat   *Poem*
Your body a bright lake seen between houses catching the
    morning sun
Pale lilies-of-the-valley in the darkness of your thighs

I've had 3 new prs. of boots since I met you   *Boots*
And I keep thinking perhaps I should get a new relationship
    as well
But I don't need to:
Perhaps it's the kind that doesn't wear out.

                                                      Lawn
I think of you
Even when walking with beautiful girls
On the lawn of rich men's houses at night
Where the sky is mowed every morning
And the stars are switched on when the guests arrive

Kisses   *Commercial*
    better for headaches than Aspirin alone.

"I'm going to London tomorrow" you said   *Spring Poem*
"And it will be Spring"   *for*
But that was last night   *Heather*
And today it's snowing.

Wind blowing inland from the Pierhead   *Liverpool*
I was glad to be seen with you in Liverpool *Poem*
Dead ferryboats in the shadows between your hair and cheek.

The New, Fast, Automatic Daffodils

(New variation on Wordsworth's "Daffodils")

I wandered lonely as
THE NEW, FAST DAFFODIL
   FULLY AUTOMATIC
that floats on high o'er vales and hills
The Daffodil is generously dimensioned to accommodate four
   adult passengers
10,000 saw I at a glance
Nodding their new anatomically shaped heads in sprightly
   dance
Beside the lake beneath the trees
   in three bright modern colours
red, blue and pigskin
The Daffodil de luxe is equipped with a host of useful
   accessories
including windscreen wiper and washer with joint control
A Daffodil doubles the enjoyment of touring at home or
   abroad

in vacant or in pensive mood
SPECIFICATION:
   Overall width   1.44 m (57")
   Overall height   1.38m (54.3")
   Max. speed   105 km/hr (65 m.p.h.)
    (also cruising speed)
DAFFODIL
   RELIABLE – ECONOMICAL
DAFFODIL
   THE BLISS OF SOLITUDE
DAFFODIL
   The Variomatic Inward Eye
Travelling by Daffodil you can relax and enjoy every mile of
   the journey.

(Cut-up of Wordsworth's poem plus Dutch motor-car leaflet)

Holcombe Poem/
Poem for a Girl I Didn't Meet

walking on the moors thinking about how I didn't meet you
    yesterday
heather underfoot and mist over Pendle
the moor changing like an animal/brown to green grey to
    purple with the weather
sky blue at the edges
               like a letter that came too late.

. . .Undine rising from the waters her golden hair
dripping in the moonlight . . . dead bird on a fence blood
dripping from its neck . . . Isis searching the rushes for her
murdered lover . . . small girl with a fishingrod
in a rushing valley full of ferns . . . the last supper
followed by the Four Just Desserts . . . watching the
white mocking figure at the edge of the Dark Forest
. . . beating naked blondehaired girls with
longstemmed purple flowers . . . Osiris judging
the dead mist rising up the valley seaweed tangled
in her moonlight hair . . .

trains
   moving through valleys
chimneys
   springing from hillsides
streams
   tumbling through boulders
clouds
   tilting from the horizon
and
   me
      on the moors
thinking about the girl I never met.

Poems For Wales

1   icegreen
        mountain streams
           fresher
              than toothpaste
                cleaner tasting
                    than menthol cigarettes.

2   Gelert's grave
   used to make me cry like a baby
   now
   they're killing Vietnamese
   instead

3   standing
   looking at the landscape
   then
   signing it at the bottom
   in the snow on a petrol-station wall

4   thinking about you
   here
   in the country
   trying to spray the moon silver
   and
   only hitting the clouds

5   two lots of footprints
   through the snow
   to my room
   both of them
   mine

Country Song

"Lily of the Valley (Convalaria Majalis, fam. Liliaceae). Grows wild in N. England. Commonly cultivated. Flowers in May. Berries red when ripe. Leaves particularly poisonous because three constituents depress the heart, like Foxglove."

What are the constituents that depress the heart?
the scent of lilies in darkgreen silences under trees
milkweed and ragwort and sunshine in hedges
small flowers picked amongst trees when it's raining

A year ago
You planted lilies in the valley of my mind
There were lilies at the bottom of my garden
And ferries at the bottom of my street

Now
I sit here in sunlight with the smell of wild garlic
Trying to taperecord the sound of windflowers and celandines

Wondering
What are the three constituents that depress the heart
Without you here in the country?

Great War Poems

1   The same old soldiers walking along the same old skyline

2   Dead hand through the sandbags reaching out for the cream-and-white butterfly

3   mud/water under duckboards/mud/rats scamper in starshell darkness/mud/smell of shit and rotting bodies/mud/resting your sweaty forehead on the sandbags OVER THE TOP the first men in the lunar landscape.

4   "What did you do to the Great Whore, Daddy?"

5   Poppies slightly out-of-focus and farmcarts bringing in the peaceful dead.

6   The ghost of Wilfred Owen selling matches outside the Burlington Arcade.

7   Seafog. Red flaring lights from the shorebatteries. The roar of shells rattle of machineguns. Water running in the bilges. My feet slipping on the damp cobbles of the quayside.

8   DON'T BE VAGUE – BLAME GENERAL HAIG.

9   four white feathers clutched in a blood-stained envelope

10 a skull nestling in a bed of wild strawberries/boots mouldering green with fungus/saplings thrusting through rusting helmets/sunken barges drifting full of leaves down autumn rivers.

Wild West Poems

1 Noon:
  2 tall gunmen walking slowly towards each other down
    Mathew St.

2 *And then*
  He tied her up
  And then
  He lit the fuse to the dynamite
  And then
  And then
  AND THEN ALONG CAME JONES . . ."

(for Leiber/Stoller
and the Coasters)

3 William H. Bonney alias Billy the Kid hitches his horse to a
  parkingmeter strides through the swing doors into Yates
  Wine Lodge. Barmaids slowly back away from the counter.
  Drunks rush out into Charlotte Street. He drinks a glass of
  Aussie White and strides out, silent as he came.

4 *Poem for Black Bart to Leave Behind on a Stagecoach*

  I hope you ladies ain't afraid
  Of the wicked man who made this raid
  But I'm like nature quick and cruel
  Believe me, gals, I need them jewels.

5 The Daltons riding down Church Street/Bullets ricochet
  off streetsigns/windows full of cardboard Walkers bottles
  shatter/Bob Grat Emmett thunder across trafficlights at
  red/hoofbeats die away clattering down Lord Street.

Hello Adrian

(*for Adrian Mitchell*)

Hello Adrian,
     This is me, Adrian. I hope you had a nice Christmas as it
finds us here. We had that nice Mr and Mrs Johnson to tea
who's president of something but they didn't like those
yellow people from across the road. Christmas had us a bit
worried but Santaclaus in his big Red Cloak came down her
chimney and now all those cards with cribs on won't be in
bad taste after all. Very strange things have been happen-
ing lately. People keep falling off cliffs and into bed with
me. Last night I met Paul McCartney in a suburban garden
wearing a moustache drawn by Marcel Duchamp. I keep
wanting to sign shelves of tins in Supermarkets. Everytime
I go for coal the coalplace is full of dead Vietcong. Birds have
eaten the berries off our plastic holly. I think it's going to be
a hard winter.
     Today is New Year's Day, should Auld Acquaintance be
Forgot? I don't know but my stomach feels funny. I have
sent messages to the leaders of the various parts of my body
asking them to end the fighting NOW. There's no shillings
left in the meter we'll have to roast a leg of pork over the
gasfire. Someone's left the front door open O My God we
might have had thieves murderers nutters queers anyone
coming up here. Now someone's taken the cat and left a
shovel instead.
     People keep offering me nebulous schemes for making
my fortune in various of The Arts. A girl told me "I had a
dreadful time on Christmas Day, Uncle Gerald kept putting
his hand up my skirt." There were huge punch-ups in
Woolworths on Christmas Eve. I have seen the entire
Works of Charles Dickens on the telly this Christmas. . .
Oliver Twist going to see Miss Havisham with Tiny
Tim . . . Scrooge skating with Mr Pickwick . . . Pip steal-
ing handkerchiefs to give to Little Nell . . . I can't stand it
any longer if those Chuzzlewits call again we're *definitely*

83

not at home. I'm making New Year Resolutions again but I'm not likely to meet her *this* year either. I'm going to have my poems on Cash's Woven Nametapes put inside school-girls' gymslips. I'm going to treat white Rhodesians as equals. I've forgotten all the others already.

I think Spring must be coming. She brought me a bunch of plastic violets yesterday. I can hear the noise of the ice floes breaking up on the bathroom floor. There's still no one waiting by the waterfall: I looked again today.

I really must close now as the Last Post is sounding, so hoping this finds you as it leaves me love to all at No.18 from all at No. 64.

Adrian

Song of Affluence *or* I Wouldn't Leave My 8-Roomed House for You

I wouldn't leave my little 8-roomed house for you
I've got one missus and I don't want two

I love you baby but you must understand
That feeling you's fine and kissing you's grand
But I wouldn't leave my little wooden wife for you

Water tastes fine but money tastes sweeter
I'd rather have a fire than a paraffin heater
And
I wouldn't change my little 8-roomed life for you.

Peter Pan Man

When I was three I went to the end of the road to watch the
    King go by
there was a lot of people and someone in a plumed hat.
When I was six, I wore a striped woolly pullover and lived at
    the seaside
somewhere, far-off, people died in the streets.
When I was eight I volunteered to join the army
tin hat, corkgun and all,
and received a nice letter from the Colonel
(". . . wait until you're old enough,
and apply through the usual channels")
When I was thirteen I drew triumphant cartoons
showing weary Japs emerging from the ruins of Hiroshima.
When I was eighteen my horizon was bounded by Cézanne
    and T.S. Eliot.
After that I missed almost everything
(though vaguely aware of Bill Haley and the War in Korea)
Until suddenly, and too late, I put away childish things
painted HANDS OFF SUEZ on walls and cried as the tanks rolled
    into Hungary
marched on marches and sat down on demos
saw people under horsehoofs
was thrown into horseboxes by reluctant policemen.
Stalin, the Uncle Joe we sang about in the war
crashed from his pillar and lay at one with the dust
The Yanks, who gave me chewing gum and nylons to
    peroxide girls
no longer F.D.R. but J.F.K., red against the green of Deeley
    Plaza
and photos of black men torn by police-dogs
I drew votive images of Guevara
and mourned for the childhood dead in Spain
Trotsky, Bakunin and Mao told me
I didn't grow up I grew down
worried about the things I never saw as a child
(though I was told off once for laughing at

mufflered clothcapped men searching for a lost sixpence
and can remember hearing rows about money
I wasn't supposed to hear).
Yes, I'm the Peter Pan Man, the Boy Who Never Grew Up
Girls didn't like me
until
Wendy laid me gratefully under an oak tree when I was 21
Since I was 35 a hundred Tinkerbells have opened their pale
    magic thighs for me
But
Captain Hook, no longer Stanley Baldwin or Winnie with his
    big cigar
Waits in the wings, his teeth bared in a TV Colgate smile
plans to take away the medicines, drink the children's milk,
imprison my brother workers.
At the gates of Halewood and St Helens
The Lost Boys argue furiously
not hearing the steady ticking of the Crocodile
black homburg and toothbrush moustache
munching black men with tears in his eyes.
And a hundred bowler-hatted briefcase Pirates
tear down the streets of the Liverpool I love
clutching their plans exultantly,
The Wendy-House is blotted out by the dust of falling
    Georgian buildings
While I sing love-poems through microphones at Festivals.
The faithful Nana has been given the humane killer
her meat makes other dogs bounce with health.
Yes Mr & Mrs Darling sold us all down the line
in 1921 and '23 and '37
in '44 and '45 and all those times since
It's me and Tinkerbell and a few of the Boys
on our own now
Crouched behind rainbow barricades of broken promises.

On the Late Late Massachers Stillbirths and Deformed Children a Smoother Lovelier Skin Job

The seven-day beauty plan:
Avenge O Lord thy slaughter'd saints, whose bones
Will cause up to 1 million deaths from leukaemia
Forget not, in thy book record their groans
Now for the vitally important step. Cream your face and neck
    a second time
No American president world-famous for beauty creams
responsible for the freedom and safety of so many young
    offenders
TODAY'S MEN OF ACTION
The Triple Tyrant Macmillan Kennedy Watkinson
The West governments are satisfied as to the moral necessity
    to resume Racing from Newmarket
EXTRA SPECIAL!
Atmospheric testing: A test card is shown
continuously from 10 a.m. until 15 minutes
before slayn by the bloody Piemontese
why pay higher fares?
There is always trouble when President Kennedy the jovial
    gravel-voiced little sailor
defends glamorous Olive Oyl from contamination of the
    atmosphere
EXTRA MONEY their moans
The Vales redoubled to the Hills
Another fire blazes in the city of London AND ALL THAT JAZZ
Do you draw your curtains with a walking-stick?
The mutation was caused by a heavy dose of radiation
    received
by the Mother at Hiroshima
This baby's eyes and nose had merged into
one misshapen feature in the middle of its
forehead lost 6" from Hips
sufferers can now wear fashion stockings

Early may fly the Babylonian wo
followed by
TOMORROW'S WEATHER
The Epilogue
close down.

Cut-up of John Milton Sonnet XV On the late
Massacher in Piemont/TV Times/CND leaflet.

The Blazing Hat, Part Two

This is the morning that we burnt a cardboard hat
flames licking the inside of the brim
This is the morning that the thunder hung like great black
    flags over the city
stirred by gusts of wind
This is the morning that they opened a new motorway
leading from my house to yours
This is the morning that I decided I wasn't getting enough
    roughage
and went on a diet of broken milkbottles
This is the morning that Death left her cloak behind
after the party
This is the morning that a beautiful schoolgirl woke me with a
    cup of coffee
in a vision
This is the morning that we saw
words written on water
This is the morning that beautiful girls with Renaissance faces
    played Hindemith records
at dawn
This is the morning after the night
before
This is the morning after the night
had strewn Canning Street with purple toiletrolls

88

This is the morning that we saw a 4-year-old boy
whipping an imaginary blonde lovely
This is the morning that Death was a letter
that was never scented
This is the morning that the poet reached out for the rolled-up
    Financial Times
followed by a dreadful explosion
This is the morning that you woke up 50 miles away seeing
    sunlight on the water
and didn't think of me
This is the morning that I bought 16 different kinds of artificial
    lilies-of-the-valley
all of them smelling of you
This is the morning that we sat and talked
by the embers of the blazing hat.

Pictures from an Exhibition

(Painting and Sculpture of a Decade '54-'64, Tate Gallery, London
    April-June 1964)

No. 54   Jean Dubuffet, "Déclinaison de la Barbe" I, 1959
"as-tu cueilli les fleurs de la barbe?"
Jean Dubuffet I wander the dark pebbles of your mind picking
    beardflowers.

No. 73   Joseph Cornell, "Hôtel de l'Étoile"

cool pillars of the hotel/in the
night outside the stars are always
so white/the sky is always so
blue/silver moon waiting patiently.

No. 84 Mark Rothko, "Reds – No. 22", 1957

SCARLET
ORANGE
ORANGE
ORANGE
SCARLET
CRIMSON
SCARLET

No. 291 Robert Rauschenberg, "Windward", 1963

printed oranges are painted
painted oranges are painted

Angry skyline over the gasworks
A Hawk sits brooding inside a painted rainbow.

**Nos. 10-13 Josef Albers, Studies for "Homage to the
Square", 1961-2**

look.

see.

long ago.

now.

**No. 314 Bernard Requichot, "Sans Titre – Chasse de papiers
choisis"**

chasse aux papillons:
"Here Be Tygers" –
– the fruit in the tin has a thousand eyes.

No. 349 Jim Dine, "Black Bathroom No.2", 1962

black splashes on the white walls
interrupting the commercials
TURN ON THE GLEAMING WHITE SINK
AND POEMS COME OUT OF THE TAPS!

No. 139   Victor Vasarely, "Supernovae", 1959-61

BLACK IS WHITE
BLACK IS WHITE
WHITE IS BLACK
WHITE IS BLACK

No. 50   Louise Nelson, "Sky Cathedral III", 1960

Black
  Black
Black
  Boxes
Black
  Light
Black
  Moonlight
Black
  Emptiness
Black
  Dust
Black
  Boxes
Black
  Black
Black

No. 247   Richard Diebenkorn, "Ingleside", 1963

Look through the Supermarket window/up the highway
the hill rises steeply/hoardings and magnolias bright
in the sunlight/white walls black freeways trafficsigns
at intersections/green lawns dark hedges/colours
clear and bright as the packets in your wire basket.

Poem in Memoriam T.S. Eliot

I'd been out the night before & hadn't seen the papers or the
   telly
& the next day in a café someone told me you were dead
And it was as if a favourite distant uncle had died
old hands in the bigstrange room/new shiny presents at
   Christmas
and I didn't know what to feel.

For years I measured out my life with your coffeespoons

Your poems on the table in dusty bedsitters
Playing an L.P. of you reading on wet interrupted January
   afternoons

Meanwhile, back at the Wasteland:
Maureen O'Hara in a lowcut dress staggers across Rhyl sand-
   hills
Lovers in Liverpool pubs eating passionfruit
Reading Alfred de Vigny in the lavatory
Opening an old grand piano and finding it smelling of curry
THE STAR OF INDIA FOUND IN A BUS STATION
Making love in a darkened room hearing an old woman
   having a fit on the landing
The first snowflakes of winter falling on her Christmas poem
   for me in Piccadilly Gardens
The first signs of spring in plastic daffodils
on city counters

Lovers kissing
Rain falling
Dogs running
Night falling

And you "familiar compound spirit" moving silently down
   Canning St in a night of rain and fog.

Where'er You Walk

"Where'er you walk
Cool gales shall fan that glade"

The Pierhead where you walked will be made a park
restricted to lovers under 21
Peasants will be found merrymaking after the storm in
    Canning St
where you walked
The station where we first arrived at night
Will be preserved for the nation
With the echo of your footsteps still sounding in the empty
    roof

"Where'er you tread
The Blushing flower shall rise"

The alleyway where we read poems to dustbins
after closing time
The kitchens where we quarrelled at parties
The kitchen where two strangers first kissed at a party
full of strangers
The ticketbarrier where we said goodnight so many times
The cobblestones in front of the station
The pub where the kindly old waiter
Always knows what we want to drink –
ALL SHALL BURST INTO BLOOM
SPROUTING FLOWERS BRIGHTER THAN PLASTIC ONES IN
    WOOLWORTH'S
Daffodils and chrysanthemums, rhododendrons and snow-
    drops, tulips and roses
– cobblestones bursting with lilies-of-the-valley

"And all things flourish"

Whole streets where you walk are paved with soft grass
so the rain will never go through your shoes again

Zebracrossings made of lilies
Belishabeacons made of orangeblossom
Busstops huge irises
Trafficlights made of snapdragons

"Trees where you sit
Shall crowd into a shade"

even in Piccadilly
stations covered in flowers yellow like the paint you once got
    in your hair
Oaktrees growing everywhere we've kissed
Will still be there when I've forgotten what you look like
And you don't remember me at all
Copies of your letters to me on blue paper
Written on the sky by an aeroplane over all the cities of
    england
Copies of your poems stamped on eggs instead of lions
We will walk forever in the darkness under fernleaves

"Trees where you sit
shall crowd into a shade"

Spring Song for Mary

"Lovers twain that cannot wed,
Praising much the greenwood bough,
Where our love may shelter now,
Praising all the leaves that shade us,
Praising, Praising, love that made us . . ."
Dafydd ap Gwilym, "The Nightingale in the Birch-Thicket"

echoing birdsong in the dark morning
nightingale from the
birch-thickets of childhood
waking me
distant cuckoofilled woods
in the city lamplight dawn
outside my window

February sunlight slants across swollen fields flooded streams
remembering the smell of your hair tangled against lilac
    sheets
Smoke from chimneystacks frozen in the sky
remembering summer thighs under your thin white dress
Sky reflected in lorrytracks through muddy buildingsites
neonsigns reflected in your eyes when we kissed in a taxi
Tiny flecks of rain on the window
young body pale in the autumn evening
Riverbanks bursting
warm mouth shining white teeth
Waves flowing across ploughed fields
my hands under your dress finding you suddenly needing me

rain moulting grey from
clouds hanging ragged from
the horizon
empty morning beaches
the silence inside ancient castles
suddenly remembering
running laughing with my friends in the summer wood
writing your name and mine
on a huge oak tree in soft crumbling chalk

train rattling my pen as I write
light birchtrees against sullen woods
wind changing the sea from blue to green
like your eyes
barges drifting on quiet canals

Come close and say the world's at an end
and me with you
There's no tomorrow, just today
Yes, come closer

tall
pylons
into the melting
afternoon
no
blue
envelope
in the morning
hallway
climbing
the abbey steps
near
where you slept
last night
coffee stained
tablecloths
on trains
cries
of seagulls
in your seablue
eyes
small
houses
huddle the hills
from
colliery valleys
warm
touch
of your mouth

96

in the secret kitchen
bright
bridgelights
in the echoing
Severn
night

"Grant us a day my love and me,
Now love's in blossom on every tree"

– Dafydd ap Gwilym

Sitting on a train
Wondering will daffodils and rhododendrons stand against
   the cruel bayonets
Will telling my love for you change the Universe?
Will telling you walking to school in winter morning darkness
cold in your brown uniform
Keep the Napalm from one frightened child?
Will telling the feel of you under my hands
bring back to life the murdered poet?

Can the thin branches stop the melting snow flooding the
   rivers?
Can my poems become food for the starving of Africa and
   Asia?
Can fieldmice and birdsnests survive the mighty earth-
   movers?
Foxes and badgers, thrushes and nightingales
take back the countryside?
Gleaming fish swim up our polluted rivers again?
Only take this song
As the factories break the skyline
As the overhead wires sing for us
As the skidding motorway tyres
scream your name with their last breath
As the evening snowlight falls on a city street
My pen tracing these words on thin yellow paper

Take
this song.

CITY

"I hear your voice vibrate in all the worlds noises"

"Her dreams in broad daylight
Make suns evaporate"

Paul Éluard, "Capitale de la Douleur"

*"Swarming city
city full of dreams
where the ghost in broad daylight
passes by the passers-by."*

Edinburgh Sept. 1967 – Liverpool Sept. 1968

PART ONE

Got up went to the telephone bought some pies and rolls for
lunch thinking of you tried to phone you they said you
weren't there came home made some coffee had my lunch
thinking of you.

Got washed put stuff under my arms to make me smell nice
thinking of you got shaved put on aftershave to make me
smell nice thinking of you listened to a record of Pannalal
Ghosh playing the flute went out into the dry city afternoon
thinking of you thinking of you.

Waking up with a headache from the night before thinking of
you feeling suddenly sick not knowing where you are no
way of talking to you no way of hearing from you Andy
thinking I'd written a Haiku without knowing it and then
discovering I hadn't.

Listening to Nadia sing "All My Trials, Lord" in the spotlit
church darkness thinking about the fresh downycheeked
slightly blushing still schoolgirl girl who used to sing it four
years ago still thinking of you.

Looking from the train window going small green fields
glimmering like a pond with lapwings golden down on the
mountainsides against a pale blue sky thinking of you
coming back orderly rows of firtrees small rows of round
trees fading into the horizon toy cars running up an
inclined slope into the mist seeing wet platforms in Carlisle
thinking of you sky and embankment covered with ferns
and brambles grey seen through a green filter writing this
poem thinking of you thinking of you.

Waking and reaching out in the early morning for the warm
bigeyed girl who called everyone a machine and whose full
breasts were a sleeping machine and whose big warm
mouth was a kissing machine and whose hot suddenly
wanting morning body a love machine I couldn't control
still thinking of you.

Drinking whisky with Hamish after a quarrel in the illicit
sundaymondaymorning hours listening to song after Celtic
song thinking of you eating a farewell meal with John and
Lucy in the latenight café we go to every night thinking of
you.

Listening to Adrian telling me about the lies they tell me about
Vietnam thinking of you thinking about the napalmed
children not flower children but innocent flowers of flame
listening to a piper playing "Lament for the Children"
listening to Simpson playing pibroch "Dargai" wondering
why I can't write a lament for the firechildren of Vietnam as
beautiful as the haunted landscape music echoing from
peak to peak and range to range of sound across glens of
silence ageless lament of the mothers for the children of the
first "pacification".

Listening to Mike read listening to Alan and Pete Morgan
listening to my friends tell me the truth thinking of you
listening to Ted Joans laughing spade hero hipster black
flower from Africa feeding the audience poems songs

chocolate and astonishment thinking of you thinking of you.

Thinking of you in the 2 a.m. slightly drunk darkness at the top of the hill with Jim and Andy seeing old and new town spread out in points of light beneath us under the towering stonehenge Doric columns the sound of a flute breaking into the still air Bartok and Debussy moving out over the lamplit streets all night railwaystation and sleeping town.

Thinking of you drinking in the latenight empty hotel lounge with Patrick newlymet friend but familiar face from the telly making takeover bids for the songs of Catullus and power struggles for control of Virgil's "Georgics".

Thinking of you trying to finish this poem back in Liverpool where everyone's my friend except some of my friends taking the flower painting I did for you to be framed in gold like our love should be thinking of you trying to finish this poem at the seaside walking with the dog along the early September already winter promenade where we walked a year ago thinking of you trying to finish this poem walking in the country a few late flowers and blackberries in the hedges the hills ahead "the spectre of repopulation" waiting huge hawkheaded just behind the skyline.

Thinking of you then one day an unexpected phone call in the afterlunchtimedrinking helping another girl to buy flowers afternoon hearing your familiar halfforgotten voice sad but still warm faraway saying you can't see me walking home with no mac and my shoes are sneakers and let the rain in everyone over 30 has shoes and an overcoat except me feeling the still warm September rain soaking through my clothes thinking of you thinking of you.

Thinking of you watching Magic Roundabout me here and you miles away hoping Florence and the boys will look after you Dougal will trip over himself trying to help Mr

McHenry will bring you flowers but Zebedee doesn't tell us
"time for bed" anymore.

Walking through dead leaves in Falkner Square going to the
Pakistani shop with Tony in the October afternoon
sunlight thinking of you being woken up in the two a.m.
Blue Angel rockn'roll darkness by Carl who I hadn't heard
singing thinking of you thinking of you drinking in the
Saturday night everyone waiting no party pub walking
with another girl holding cold hands in the autumn park
thinking of you walking home everynight in Blackburne
Place twilight thinking of you thinking of you.

PART TWO

november.

the long fog echoes in from the river.

9.30

echoing schoolgirl hymnsinging voices into the mist outside
Blackburne House

leaves.

Ted and me eating Chinese roast duck in the November
afternoon.

foghorns

Beautiful angel who couldn't open the door

kissing warm mouth hard teeth eyes shining like the river
where the jetty puts out to sea in lines of lights

season of nice tits and hollow uselessness

cold streets.

meat oozing electric blood on hard white counters

tossing your red-gold hair your black
cloak flying
your witcheyes laughing

frost at midnight.

the lone hydrangea holding out against the guns of winter

halfremembered kisses on the tip of my tongue

cold wind straining against the windowframe

thinking of you

thinking of you

A550	Hawarden	light like pale golden marmalade
	Penyffordd	thrown against the road and sky
A5104	Llandegla	red leaves falling into our headlights
	Corwen	
A494	Bala	the immobile lake extends its
		sleeping waters
	Dolgellau	under the long glory of a winter moon
A487	Machynlleth	waves glowing pale blue in the
		darkness
	Aberstwyth	dark figures of my friends running
		along the curving promenade

factories at Widnes and Runcorn ravishing through the mist

orange Turner sunsparks on the grey river

red spot on the train window earth mist colours of autumn
    landscape

loudspeakers in Crewe

pale lemon light through the dark fringed conifers on the
    horizon

dinky cars bowling along the motorway

winter sunlight slanting across fields

sun through mist hurting my eyes

frozen ferns tall grass and umbelliferous plants
etched with white

thinking of you thinking of you

lamplight on hard frozen station platforms

Tintern Abbey looming out of the morning
(remembering dark eyes . . .)

and the Abbey Café
(D. and W. Wordsworth, proprietors)

spotlights playing over warm purple soft green trees

suddenly the long brown river
currents plaiting its sides

paleblue trees resting on the other side

fishermen

and one broken bridge
Chinese in the distance

ploughed fields Paul Nash hills coming up out of the mist

eggs for breakfast in Southampton
hardboiled to eat on the train

industrial watchtowers looming out of the morning

huge Martian head peering over buildings

falling into the train then washing
boiling water coming out of the tap marked COLD

running over station bridges with whistles blowing

jumping out of taxis into trains just starting
bruising my knee
thinking of you

missing connections
waiting on stations everywhere

running over more bridges
carrying my life inside a leather briefcase

missing connections
the railways winning on frozen points

stopping me
catching trains
coming to see you

waiting for a taxi
the morning your last phonecall came

104

thinking of you
thinking of you

coming home

cat waiting black bigeyed in the hall
for Kit-E-Kat

going out again

leaving her rolled up sleeping
warm catdreams on the settee

thinking of you
thinking of you

PART THREE

here
in another Welsh landscape
rain
creeping quietly over the grass
through the window

thinking
of
you
coming up the path
to my
room
in the November sunset
red sky
between
clumps of trees and clouds dark
against Moel Fammau

cheerful light
in the November bathroom

105

Landscape, Golden Valley

Arthur Giardelli   viii · 1980

coming back
2 years later
thinking of

            you laughing lying in the bath
                  face downwards
             paddling in the shallows
               body pink and white
                   glowing
             green and white tiles
                  red towel
      through the steam on my glasses
           soft brown bodyhair
          flowing like waterweed

now

the tiles still cutting back
in small diamonds
to the window
in the strong March daylight

furniture still the same

creampainted chest-of-drawers
          (your pink
         nightdress in
            the
3rd drawer down
creampainted iron beds
        (paint
        peeling in places
creampainted walls
curtains and bedcover
        green folkweave
blackpattern diagonal
some sounds of you
still there
among all the footsteps

muddy boots
on the floor
from long walks
along the footpath
along the cliffedge
with the daylight fading
or
on our last night there
after making love
you sleeping peacefully
me looking for a lost girl

nervous voices   torches   searching
        cold rain   dripping trees
      holding the other girl's hand
          in the secret darkness
              smelling of you

                    lost
              girl found
            foot of the cliff
          in the early morning
      huddled   crumpled   hair matted
        freckled with blood and mud
      the haunted eyes of a Bellmer doll

you
slipping
out
at dawn
for the last time
rain
sweeping in from the hills

coming back
in another year
in Springtime
thoughts

of
you
straying   sheep
in the gardens
outside the window
clouds
lifting from the horizon
thinking of
you
in
another room

shadows
lengthening across the valley

your little dancing step
backwards
as you open the door
pink lacy knitted sweater
(pink nylon seethru bra
small soft breasts underneath)
blue skirt
black furry slippers
hair tied back
laughing invitation
dancestep backwards
opening the darkred door
at the end of the yellow corridor

coming through the door
coming for dinner
steam on the windows
dark trees   lamplight outside
one red   one blue
plastic soupbowl
out ready on the table
closing the door then standing on tiptoe to kiss me
hands

feeling the curve
of your white nylon panties
under the skirt
sometimes not waiting
to eat
undressing each other
seeing
the familiar
underwear
body
always
for the first time
out
in the morning
hiding like naughty children
till the landlord goes out
watching for the grey car
in the driveway
(Breakfast
with Radio Caroline
eggs
or cornflakes
in the red and blue bowls again)
little room
room with posters covering the walls
room like you
room that looks like you smells like you
room like me
room with too many blankets in summer
room with gasfire in winter
room that means we don't have to make love in an alleyway
green lane at night on the way to your bus station
room where we pick up our clothes afterwards
room tidy now for coffee
room happy sitting back feeling tired
room you smiling at me from the gas stove
room five to twelve our happy bodies
room sleep now till morning hoping we meet no one at the
    bus-stop

110

room gone now
room preserved forever
because of you
because of me
because we wrote down one night everything in it
because it looked like you
even when you weren't there
room rented now like my dreams
to someone else

here
now
in our other room
March sunlight gone over the hills
line of lights down the drive
to the publichouse electric
where I'm going tonight with someone else
alone in the bathroom
thinking
of you
thinking
of
you

PART FOUR

(for G.A. and M.D.)

East Berlin
May 1968

Walking along the Unter den Linden
thinking of you smelling the green
from the lindenleaves

church steps still pockmarked with bulletholes

tiny shining watercolour worlds of Emil Nolde
Tahitian girls basking in the sunshine
menaced by the angry sea

111

on the mantelpiece

29 Grove Park
off Lodge Lane
Liverpool 8
15th September 1966

1 travelling-clock at ten to twelve
1 Ever-Ready U14 gas lighter
half a packet of elastic bands
Pot of Nivea
Jar of Pond's Cold Cream ("The 7-day Beauty Plan 42 gms
    net")
Max Factor Eye Makeup Removal Pads
1 packet Sungold "Colaire"
Pond's "Fresh Start" New Medicated Cleansing Gel
Body Mist Aerosol Perfume Spray
Body Mist Lemon Bouquet Spray
two not very sharp pairs of scissors
1 postcard of a flowerpiece by Bonnard
Coty "L'Aimant" Hand Lotion
Coty "L'Aimant" Skin Perfume
1 postcard "In the Forest" by Douanier Rousseau
1 postcard of a Dubuffet mindscape
my keys to her flat
leather purse
Rentbook with 21 weeks paid
a fountain pen (black)
small Tupperware container with 7 shillings for the gasfire
tube of Anadin (7 left)

le Thil-Manneville
par Gueures
Seine-Maritime
France

Pink flowers   green bushes   against whitewash wall
feet sliding through soft wet chalk
pale violet hydrangeas crowding in at the night lavatory
    window
landscapes
wheat   flax   barley   oats
cornfields bright for Ford Madox Brown
fields bright with tractors   combineharvesters
    orange   red   yellow

on the gas stove

1 kettle, almost boiling, on rear right-hand gas burner
1 empty saucepan, used for thick Lincoln Pea Soup
1 fryingpan

*poem instead of
a photograph
for John and Ann*

green   grass
dappled with darkgreen shadow
empty winebottles   tablecloth   pale orange melonrinds
Ann pink towelling dress   against darkgreen bushes
holding Esther in pale violet dress
one pink flower in the background

on the table

1 tinopener with bottle-opening device
1 empty pint bottle No. 1 Strong Ale
top of the bottle
2 empty glasses
2 empty coffee mugs (one brown one green)
1 lilac ribbon
small mirror
1 box Kleenex
The "Devon Comfy" handmade comb
1 tail comb in green nylon

*Varengeville
(for Mike and Jenny)*

Cliffs white stained with red and ochre
white stones
sitting up like seabirds
lying like sealions
crowned with fringecaps of wet green hair
heads of Frankenstein monsters buried in the sand

113

on the armchair

1 pair white nylon panties
1 "no-bra" bra
1 pair stocking tights
1 vest dyed navyblue
1 green corduroy skirt
1 pr. gents khaki denim trousers
1 gents polo-necked black sweater with paintstains

Translating a poem Guillaume wrote for you:

My dear little Lou	I love you
My dear little trembling star	I love you
Body so beautifully supple	I love you
Deep cavern that squeezes like a nutcracker	I love you
Left nipple so pink and cheeky	I love you
Right nipple so delicately rosy	I love you
Right breast like champagne before it's bottled	I love you
Left breast like the forehead of a newborn calf	I love you
Inner lips swollen with too frequent loving	I love you
Rounded cheeks moving exquisitely sticking out so proudly behind you	I love you
Pubic hair blonde as a winter forest	I love you
Navel like a dark lunar crater	I love you
Armpits downy like a newborn cygnet	I love you
Delicate slope of your shoulders	I love you
Thighs whose roundness is as beautiful as the columns of ancient temples	I love you
Ears veined like tiny Mexican jewels	I love you
Hair drenched in the blood of love	I love you
Knowing feet feet that tense themselves	I love you
Loins that straddle me loins so powerful	I love you
Figure that has never needed a girdle slender figure	I love you
Back so marvellously shaped curving itself for me	I love you
Mouth where I drink delights	I love you
Onenandonly glance starglance	I love you

114

Hands whose movements I adore   I love you
Nose so aristocratic   I love you
The way you walk dancing like a wave breaking   I love you
O little Lou   I love you   I love you   I love you

on the drainingboard

1 plastic container full of Nescafé
1 tin Marvel instant non-fat milk
1 Pyrex Mixer
blue plastic teastrainer
2 facecloths 2 tablets Lux toiletsoap
1 dishcloth
1 plastic container with green Wisdom toothbrush and
2 partly-used tubes of Euthymol toothpaste
1 stainless-steel Empire teaspoon
1 practically empty 2/-Squeezy
1 almost empty bottle Goddess Extra-Rich Luxury Shampoo

Mr A. Henri
c/o Logan
6 Summerside Place,
Leith,
Edinburgh,
Scotland.

Thinking of you
seeing again the remembered
flat roof   stonebuilt houses
garden wall   flowerbeds
lilactree and lawn
sky lowering

in a large C&A bag on the floor (for washing)

1 pr. black-and-white nylon panties
1 pr. pink and white Broderie Anglaise panties
1 pr. flowered panties
2 prs. red gingham panties
1 pr. blue gingham panties
3 prs. black stretch nylon panties
1 pr. nylon stockings

Walking a year from when this poem was started
Summer into autumn railings not green grass
dried leaves trailing scraping along the pavement
eddying in the autumn wind at streetcorners
walking to the Sunday shops with her scarf wound round
    against the cold

on the floor

electric iron
raffia shoppingbasket
1 silver PVC shoppingbasket containing
oil pastels a rubber etc.
1 brush in a plastic cup of turpentine
2 pr. ladies black shoes
2 pr. ladies blue shoes
1 pr. white leather boots
1 pr. gents black chelsea boots
1 pr. canvas sneakers
1 pr. black nylon fur slippers
1 wrist watch at five to twelve
1 pale blue nylon nightdress

Living now with another girl warm welcoming at five to
midnight lopsided teddybear in a knitted overall round
thighs darkblue panties head uplifted in pubs laughing

on the bed

1 almost new Dutch blanket
2 pillows
tangled sheets and blankets
2 people 1 male 1 female

THINK

116

Sydney Jeremy Nadia churchsongs castle slung theatrical
against the sky

THINK

Garden Flat
47 Downshire Hill
London, N.W.3

sitting finishing this poem
sunlight on Hampstead morning garden
green grass   light through leaves
white posts   one red rose
trying to forget you taking away part of me
then giving it away   shadows
chasing sunlight across the breakfast garden
Bodymist starglance leaves taxis stations
frost greenandwhite lino warmth soupbowls
one pink flower a flute Night city they said
you weren't there   1 black nylon bra (on the
armchair) fading over the hills cliffs daylight
frost   voices   darkness   smelling of you

THINKING

remembered bulletholes dappled with darkgreen shadows
echoing into the mist Nadia singing wet green hair
empty hotel lounge   seeing you for the last time
or was it the time before streets a bridge junkshops
bringing you a Beatles record for Christmas wanting
to tell you what's in this poem and can't Guillaume
combineharvesters clouds Welsh landscape (pink
nightdress) standing on tiptoe cliffedge daylight
searching Chinese bridges pagoda roast duck
railings   hair flying   leaves dripping
THINKING OF

stonebuilt houses Nolde girls green sea empty landscapes
cliffs stained with ochre 2 coffeemugs 1 white 1 green

117

frost at midnight All My Trials Lord mist gantry bridge
in Lancashire town crisscross girders over wasteground
between railwaylines near-strangers holding hands
dark crumpled varnish mummy in provincial museumcase
us in the artgallery somewhere to go to for our two hours
Isis and Osiris sharing our secret five to midnight like
a winter forest floating like seaweed night hydrangeas
at the window dry city afternoon aftershave wet chalk
cornfields cornflakes the columns of ancient temples
Moel Fammau white nylon panties cold streets ferns
THINKING OF YOU

lilactree Unter den Linden the old town lights pink towelling
dress Ann seabirds Blackburne House voices in morning
fog silence on wet afternoons hair drenched her pale face
pale brown cloak in the winter park Lowry children chimney
in the distance grass dying frost factory towers waiting
room showing you the beginning of this poem (I think)
remembering the Brown Ale bottle the railway sandwiches
not what we said going out buying rolls for lunch for dinner
what we said going out buying rolls for lunch for dinner
steam on the window publichouse electric another girl
sunlight

Thinking of you

window frame   cold wind   small soft breasts newborn calf
leaves dying dripping frost at five to midnight earth
goodbye station steps the last time phonecall seaside
winter promenade sunlight on leaves train rattling through
the night landscape leaves cold wind sunlight black
nylon fur slippers songs hills room rented now like my
dreams

thinking of

pale orange violet blue nightdress on the floor grass leaves

thinking
118

dancestep backwards a wave breaking yellow corridor

think

leaves darkness sunlight smelling of you

think

drifting room

think

another girl

think

think

ing

of

th

i

nk

th

i

nk

i

ng

o

f

119

R.C.A

LIVERPOOL SCENE
TOURING USA OCT-NOV

American Representation
Dee Anthony
Bandana Enterprises Ltd
1060 Park Avenue
New York   N.Y. (212) 348-8133

Manager:
Sandy Roberton
38 Astell St London SW3

AMERICA

A Confidential Report to Dr Bertolt Brecht on the Present Condition
of The United States of America

"America, fabulous meltingpot!
God's own country!
Just called by the initials,
USA,
Like everybody's boyhood friend, incapable of change!"
– Bert Brecht, "Vanished Glory
of New York the Giant City"

TWA Flight 707 1300 hrs from London arr. NY 4.30

late pounding down pier 22   12.1V.69
blue sky soft ribbed sandclouds

Loew's Midtown Motor Inn.   8th Ave between 48th and 49th
   Streets, New York, NY 10019

sunset helicopters Hudson river
from my 11th-story window

waking to red-and-black funnels behind the buildings
noise of rockdrills police sirens waking me every morning
RHEINGOLD, THE TEN-MINUTE HEADACHE

terrible heat like an oven between the buildings   14.1X.69

On Broadway
3 black prostitutes   13.1X.69
beautiful
standing like the Supremes
about to sing "Stop
in the Name of Love"
as I walk round the corner

Al Kooper tired nervous cowboy
at home
playing the electric keyboard

The Dixie Restaurant: Closed for Jewish New Year

Television: hideous quizgames

day   Batman

and   The Addams family

night   stockmarket quotations

Castle: for Malcolm Morley

man in a sailboat
placed there by the invisible hand
motionless for ever
not wondering why
stones as real as painted clouds
at the hard white edges the dream fades
in the hard white empty studio

                              for John Clem Clarke
drifting along with the tumbling tumbleweed
in the St Adrian Co.
painted Cavaliers quietly watched me get pissed
bright lights Coney Island on Bleeker St
yellow taxi home

Pennsylvania Landscape from the Air

parallel brown treemossed hills
curving away straight like tiretracks
bluemisted to the horizon
cottonwool pinches of clouds

122

near the ground
brown slow river muddy with islands
turning highways
green/brown Stella stripes of fields
cars ponds mirrors hidden among the trees

5.X.69

WHEN IN HISTORIC VALLEY FORGE STAY AT THE GEORGE WASHINGTON MOTOR LODGE

gleaming peacock butterflywings
inside plastic blocks
in a New York shopwindow

a fly falling down vertically
before my eyes
kicked twice
and dying
whilst cleaning my teeth
in a Holiday Inn in Kent, Ohio.

5.X.69
for Allen Ginsberg

Allen stumbling walk guide to the nightworld
buying egg creams at the allnight Gem Spa
dirty faded sign FIVE-SPOT
trashcans car engines mattresses
meeting a man carrying a shining bikewheel
in dark wiremesh Tomkins Square
strange beautiful cracked voice
autoharp dulcimer songs of Innocence and Experience
lambs dancing on the hillsides
poet burying his face in the rainsoaked grass
dark streets distant glass breaking
home in a yellow taxi

the girl who sits next to me in the hotel coffeeshop
furcoat worrying about her acne eating a hot fudge sundae

Ohio Landscape from the air

patterns of township
clumps of red gold orange trees
pale clay streaked
round green ponds reflecting the sun
rows of parked cars
shining like child's glass beads in the sunlight

6.X.69

I sit on a bench on the sidewalk
outside the sad laundromat
red-and-black birds darting in cages
in the petshop next door

The poet dies, killed by the child's snowball.

NYC 21.X.69
for Jean Cocteau

wanting to give you Taglioni's jewelbox.   images for
                                                            Joseph Cornell

brown velvet
nine crystal icecubes
jewelled alladinscave
between the spaces
when you lift them out

constellations wheel
outside the windows of the Hotel de l'Univers

pharmacy:
butterflywings and histories of Cleopatra
stored on the gleaming shelves

wooden parrots yawn
in the deserted shootingallery
124

floodlit skaters in Rockerfeller Plaza
light on iceblades
dyed unreal brightgreen trees

                                        images for Mike Evans

AMERICAN WIG CO. COVERS THE WORLD

WORLD HOUSEWRECKING CO.

The Venus Brassière Co.

"what a shame they don't have Jurgens lotion in Russia"
– think of all those Red hands they could have avoided

DANTE'S INFERNO
STEAK TONIGHT

Also
Sprach Zarathustra
dawn spacemusic
for frozen breakfasts

phone call to you $32 plus tax

beautiful sad distant littlegirl voice
black cat waiting beside you in the darkened hallway

                                                28.X.69

across the Mystic bridge to Salem
blue schoolgirl's witcheyes blue stockings
past giant cactuses
leaning towers of Pizza
plaster cattle grazing on floodlit lawns

                                        Boston 17.X.69

                                            125

loving you
in identical Holiday Inn bedrooms
only the landscape outside the window
different
(changed once weekly)

1.X1.69

night landscape to NYC from the air

for the American painters of the
              1950s: MR/AR/BN

frozen tundras of cloud
caught with gold from the setting sun

dark hard horizonline
redgold edge
darktoned lakes
below the line
sprinkled with pale yellowgreen lights

bright neon jewelry
laid out on plump blackvelvet display cushions

small white things shattered at my feet twice, mysteriously
twice crossing Sheridan Square, unsure
turning to your beautiful black embrace   for Ted Joans
poetfriend from Timbuctu and Edinburgh   NYC 7.X.69

                              for Moondog
proud Norseman   Detroit 6.X1.69
standing on the corner of the Avenue of the Americas
spear horns unpraised
heavy trafficsounds
fog on the Hudson
roar of rockdrills
behind blind eyes waves of music crashing through his head

126

"But
Now, to get jobs, the 22-year-old
Girls sniff cocaine before going out
to win a place at the typewriter"

– Brecht, "New York"

Mike and I looking at the Chrysler building
and suddenly
water falling on us from the sky
people staring at us
two men dripping wet
walking down neon electric 42nd Street
on a sunny afternoon

night subway home at 3.30 people sleeping on benches

laughing brownfaced girls from New Orleans
giving us grapes on the Staten Island Ferry

night   for Brent, Tanis and Sonny
Manhattan bridgeline   Rollins. Detroit X.X1.69
hearing in my head
lonely saxophone in the night
from the Williamsburg bridge

images for James Nutt and his painting.

desolation in a Chicago hotel bedroom.

Amerika the blank staring face behind the pinball machine
eyes painted on the glass
Lake Michigan beautiful uncaring
tall towers into the night
green Frankenstein light in tunnels
painted mouth screaming soundlessly
behind the unwinking lights
orange falltrees shed their leaves sadly
along the expressways

"Ah, the women's voice from the phonographs!
So they sang (keep those records) in the Golden Age!
Euphony of the evening waters of Miami!"

– Bert Brecht

Bellefontaine, Ohio
"Monument to the 1st concrete pavement in America 1891"

INTERSTATE 75 blue-and-red highway shield

Michigan – Ohio 13.XI.69

leaves burning on suburban lawns
darkred Rothko barns white clapboard houses
familiar M1 pink homelight across evening fields

the secret storm in Columbus, Ohio

neonlights through the snowflakes
cosy porchlights through the trees
across snowcovered lawns

Sue standing at the top of the stairs
her shadow on the wall
waiting

old men trudging through leaves in the park
blind musician gone from the streetcorner for the winter
men fixing Christmastrees in front of skyscrapers

NYC 20.X.69

the poet falls
blood trickles from his head into the snow
darkred beautiful
as roses in evening gardens
between Mobile and Galveston.

Detroit 6.XI.69
for Guillaume Apollinaire

128

AUTOBIOGRAPHY

IN MEMORIAM

Albert Johnson d. May 13th, 1970
Frances Johnson, née Potter d. May 16th, 1970
Emma Henri, née Johnson d. June 3rd, 1970
Arthur Maurice Henri d. June 29th, 1970

I

knocking on the nextdoor door. knocking. no answer. knock-
ing. on their door. knocking. no answer. silence. then the
sound of something moving slowly painfully inside bumping
into things. door slowly opens. dirty matted hair dark-
shadowed crusted eyes wild growth of white hair and beard.

"who are you, then?"
the old twinkle in his redrimmed eyes
"come in, stranger."
he moves slowly ahead hobbling on brokenslippered feet
between objects too shrouded with dirt to be identified
"it's Adrian, love"
"who?"
"Adrian, your grandson, come to see you."
room dark everything covered in soot sunlight barely able to
get through the window, a small fire burning in the grate
despite the heat of the day. she sits there like some terrible
white vegetable unmoving there in her armchair: blind,
unable to move, barely able to hear. sometimes she speaks,
then dozes off again. her hands move occasionally twitch at
the blanket round her waist. the Elsan bucket next to her
dominates all the other smells in the overheated room. the
only things in her life now: being lifted on to it, being lifted off
it. sleeping. sometimes speaking to make sure you're still
alive that the other one's still there. a nurse has come to dress
his feet. she peels off the bandages. huge swollen sores on his
poor twisted feet, feet that have been good for a lifetime of

walking, working on a farm as a boy, working for the Corporation in the park across the road, pushing her in a wheelchair already semi-invalid for ten miles when they're on holiday. he seems to doze away, as well, between sentences.

yes, they're all right. just a bit tired today.

no, I can't do anything. the girl from round the corner looks in of a morning to see if we need any messages.

money? no, we're all right.

we've got plenty of food.

space cleared on the oilcloth at the front of the table; all kinds of tins and packets and old cakes pushed back, disappearing in the dirt and cobwebs and shadows at the back. finally, helpless, I get up to go.

"all right, son, it's been nice seeing you. it does her good you know.

come and see us again.

don't leave it so long, next time.

he's going now, love."

"what?"

"he's going now."

"oh, goodbye, love. Tata."

bend over to kiss her. then struggle down the filthy littered unfamiliar corridor I know from childhood. out into daylight. grass growing between the cracked pavingstones. two days later they were taken to hospital. a week later he died. three days after that she died. I go to look at him in the funeral parlour. face white, strangely peaceful but they've shaved his moustache off along with the overgrown hair. why? it isn't him. why can't they leave him alone? his flesh is waxy, unreal, slight reddish purple contusions here and there like on a newly plucked turkey at Christmas. white satin fringed with purple tucked round him. floral tributes with little cards in Cellophane packed heaped round his coffin.

PART ONE 1932-51

1

flags and bright funnels of ships
walking with my mother over the Seven Bridges
and being carried home too tired
frightened of the siren on the ferryboat
or running down the platform on the Underground
being taken over the river to see the big shops at Christmas
the road up the hill from the noisy dockyard
and the nasty smell from the tannery you didn't like going
      past
steep road that made your legs tired
up the hill from the Co-op the sweetshop the blue-and-white-
      tiled pub
Grandad's allotment on the lefthand side
behind the railings curved at the top
cobblestone path up the middle to the park
orderly rows of bean canes   a fire burning   sweetpeas tied
      up on strings
up to Our House
echoing flagyard entry between the two rows of houses
brick buttresses like lumps of cheese against the backyard
      walls
your feet clang and echo on the flags as you run the last few
      yards
pulling your woolly gloves off
shouting to show Grandad what you've just been bought
him at the door tall like the firtree in the park
darkblue suit gleaming black boots shiny silver watch chain
striped shirt no collar on but always a collarstud
heavy grey curled moustache that tickles when he picks you
      up to kiss you
sometimes shouting angry frightening you
till you see the laughter in his countryman's blue eyes

2

round redbrick doorway
yellow soapstone step cleaned twice a week
rich darkred linopattern in the polished lobby
front room with lace runners and a piano that you only go in
    on Sundays
or when someone comes to tea
Uncle Bill asleep in his chair coming in smelling of beer and
    horses
limping with the funny leg he got in the war
Grandma always in a flowered apron
the big green-and-red parrot frightening you with his sudden
    screeches
the two little round enamelled houses on either side of the
    fireplace
big turquoise flowered vase in the middle
the grate shining blackleaded cooking smell from the oven
    next to it

big black sooty kettle singing on the hob
fireirons in the hearth
foghorns and hooters
looking out of the kitchen window
seeing the boats on the bright river
and the cranes from the dockyards

3

coming back the taxidriver doesn't know where the street is
the allotments at the foot of the hill
gone now
great gaunt terraces of flats
scarred with graffiti
instead
the redbrick houses tiny falling apart

the whitewashed backyard
where you could smell lilyofthevalley through the
    privethedge round the tiny garden
on your way to the lavatory at the end
empty dirty overgrown now
backdoor banging in the wind
grandmother grandfather both dead in hospital
one windowpane broken dirty lace curtain flapping
the funny little flights of steps
the secret passages in the park
pink sandstone steps overhung with trees up the side of the
    hill
overgrown or demolished
the big seacaptain's house where I used to go for a present
    every Christmas
forgotten
remembering
lying in bed
in the dark crying listening to my mother and father argue
wind banging a shutter
indoors somewhere
dead eyes looking out from flyblown photographs
empty mirrors reflecting the silence

4

RHYL SANDS:
your vision swept clear and bright by the wind that's
    wiping away the stormclouds
beach low and empty   pale blue sky   seagulls and one dog
    near the horizon
pebbles underfoot as clear as the wallpaper in seaside cafés
somewhere out at sea, a rainbow
the sad peeling offseason colours of arcades and kiosks
David Cox's "Rhyl Sands" a tiny gem burning quietly in dirty
    Manchester
ghostly echoes of last season's chip-papers in the drifting
    sand

5

the house I lived in destroyed
now a glaring plateglass motorshowroom
only morning glories left on the fence by The Cut
narrow brickwall gorge
a thin trickle of smelly water now
not the raging torrent I once fell into coming home crying
    covered in pondweed
long low home violet slate roof two front doors with circular
    coloured windows
two garden paths big rockery border the rocks painted with
    orange spots
(I never found out why)
long rambling garden at the back with the woodyard behind
tall metal fence always coming down
whitewashed outside toilet for my lonely fantasies
echoing flagstone floor to the diningroom my mother said was
    haunted
rambling rosecovered fences lilactrees gooseberry bushes
appletree with a black cat climbing in it
Trigger the Wonderdog died aged thirteen in our new Council
    House
the old stone houses next door gone
the caravan full of noisy children
the ponies in the field across the road
the sound of donkeys distant in the brickyard field
the rusty whitewashed corrugated fence goals or wickets
by our backdoor where I used to play
gone
now
only a bald concrete patch
outside the brightlit nightglass windows

6

carrying my gasmask to school every day

buying saving stamps
remembering my National Registration Number
(ZMGM/136/3 see I can *still* remember it)
avoiding Careless Talk Digging for Victory
looking for German spies everywhere
Oh yes, I did my bit for my country that long dark winter,
me and Winston and one or two others,
wearing my tin hat whenever possible
singing "Hang out the Washing on the Siegfried Line"
aircraft-recognition charts pinned to my bedroom wall
the smell of paint on toy soldiers
doing paintings of Spitfires and Hurricanes, Lancasters and
    Halifaxes
always with a Heinkel or a Messerchmitt plunging helplessly
    into the sea in the background
pink light in the sky from Liverpool burning 50 miles away
the thunder of daylight flying fortresses high overhead
    shaking the elderberry-tree
bright barrageballoons flying over the docks
morning curve of the bay seen from the park on the hill
after coming out of the air raid shelter
listening for the "All Clear" siren
listening to Vera Lynn Dorothy Lamour Allen Jones and The
    Andrew Sisters
clutching my father's hand tripping over the unfamiliar kerb
I walk over every day
in the blackout

7

walking to the spring wood now a muddy buildersyard
footpaths then mysterious trackless intrepid
now suburban bungalowstreets gravel and tarmac
where the churnedup mud horsedung and puddles were
the woods alive with primrose and milkwort
wood-anemone and bright hawthorn
now a haven for gnomes and plastic waterfalls

8

darkgreen mysterious spaces under hedges
nettles along footpaths
to the Old Mill
stinging your legs
rubbing yourself with dock leaves
dog-rose and sweet briar
angelica and fennel
saxifrage starring the hedgerows

9

seeing into the clear water of the stream
the little wooden bridge
the fields rising on either side dusted with buttercups
darkgreen waterweed swaying
bright ripples echoed in gold below
pale brown blue grey pebbles on the pale sandy bed
eels and sticklebacks wriggling black away from your hand

10

lying on my back
listening to creeping insectsounds smelling the grass round
    me
looking at the sky
perspectives of sound
crickets   birdsong in the woods across the valley
clover ratstails celandines rabbitdroppings
feeling the movement of the earth
through my closed eyelids

11

water foaming and fizzing round your warm body
sudden rush upwards green light everywhere
sharp salty taste in your mouth your nose stinging
down again gasping your breath in
sounds rushing in cries of bathers distant children
the promenade the Pavilion bright like a postcard

12

sunlight on long grass
old lace curtains draped over raspberry canes
plump gooseberries cobwebbed in the shadows
the smell of lilac and woodfires burning
remembering the day I walked five miles to draw the waterfall
then found my pen was empty and bought a postcard with my
    last sixpence
and had to walk home
the postcard still pinned on my studio wall
frozen water falling white blood from a giant's side
walking after cocoa and buns and hearing of a poet's death on
    the radio
alone in the vast sad hospital
cowparsley patterning the hedges
light spilt like paint through the leaves

13

deep rosepetals on a close-cropt lawn
the scent of clover lying close to the earth
envious of the coolness under the green rosebush
a sad young poet thinking of her eyes the colour of shadows
    under the sycamores
shadows and a myriad insects creep in the tangled grasses
in the evening sunlight
filled with the sound of a thousand departing motorcoaches

14

remembering
the sudden pangs at corners
glimpsing the laughter of happy couples in the street
flat moonbranch shadows on the pavement
under a summer moon
or winter lamplight
nightwalks through the purgatory of half-built
    housingestates
the last-minute shifting of a cushion
for the seduction-scene that never takes place
for the waiting at the end of the privetlane
for the person who never comes

15

sad
boy-to-be-poet
head full of words
understood by no one
walking the dog
through the midnight bungalowworld
built over the
countryside
of his dreams

Poem for Hugh MacDiarmid

Dear Chris,
If I could only tell, like you
the kind of poetry I want
I write this though
I barely know you
to say "hello" to

though I have sat and listened to your song
great long river tumbling and coursing with language
leaping with huge strange unfamiliar boulders
marram-grass in the sandy wasteland
quartz-pebbles on a sloping beach
grey moustache stained yellow at the edges
laughing, drink in hand, eternal darkred tie
(tractors ploughing white phosphates in the springtime earth
    through the window)

wanting to plait my song
like you
through the streams and courses of life
to make everyone see
to make everyone know
to change the world

no more poverty
no more dying
no more illness
no more ignorance
"the air curdled with angels"
in the bloodred sunset
over the black islands of your songs.

II

ten child's eyes staring bright at the camera on the Sundaybest settee.

AVRIL   hair in curls from the rags it's rolled up in every night. me running with her pram up and down the sandhills. thin, shy, loving the cats, frightened of the gascooker. new Civil Service life, flat with Sunday dinner for me and Andy in Nottingham.

TONY   the brother I took for long walks coming back proud

140

bearing tiddlers flashing in the murky jamjar the spring lanes not yet converted to buildersyards. hitchhiking round Europe laying girls in my spare bedroom tired eyes at the dead morning railwaystation.

CHRISTINE dark beautiful once bitten by the dog now bringing my nephew to see me laughing splashing in the bath. cheeky always in trouble now a nursingsister in a country hospital.

MICHELLE brown eyes sunburnt face frilly dress. ponytail teenager dancing at parties kissing on the stairs, married in a little flat high above the busy concrete promenade.

ANDRE round plump Wimpy face fair hair neatly parted T-shirt patterned with motorcars toy cars and electric roadways patterning the floor now tall buying me pints dancing in discothèques.

me an only lonely child then suddenly a brother. brothers with toy trains bicycles and beer sisters coming to Liverpool for summer dresses or winter popstar concerts. coming home laden with parcels every Christmas. no longer knowing what will surprise them what will please them. Christmas dinner treelights wrappingpaper darkness creeping about with laden stockings making mincepies at 2 a.m. laughing with my mother. long summers of picnics on the beach and home over the humpbacked railwaybridge. new school uniforms we couldn't afford every autumn. spring offensives of whooping cough and measles. always letters from my Mum for money. train tearing me away from my childhood as I write this looking at the full breasts of the girl opposite moving slightly under the pink flowered shirt. September sun on flooded fields. me and André and Tony walking back drunk from the pub after the last funeral weekend. "Christ, we're orphans" he said, suddenly. we moved on, laughing, empty council-house full of memories waiting for us.

141

PART TWO 1951-7

1

young
artstudent
under the bridges of Paris
(where else?)
painting badlypainted picturepostcard paintings
Pont des Arts, St-Germain-l'Auxerrois
sketchbook
corduroy elbows on the Pernod table

2

crystalline manna counterpoints the stars
in the deep puddle
frost on gateposts
iridescent
a heavy Williams shadow plunges
blindly between the fuchsias the acacias and the waiting
     angels
into No. 20, Mon Repos
watched by the lonely poet
midnight dog pissing in the shadows

3

winter evening trickles cold wetness
down black glass between the curtain and the wall
fearing
the stranger's eyes behind your face
when you look too long in the mirror

4

babyfaced   almost thin   N.H.S. glasses
striped college scarf thrown casually over shoulder
various sets of artistic beards and moustaches
learning to drink
Newcastle Brown, Export and Exhibition
Saturdaynight litany of pubs with Alan from the electric train
falling headfirst down a stone colonnade at a Jazz Band Ball
seeing Orphée and Potemkin
waking drunk at 2 a.m. on the roof of someone's house
loving unhappily a greeneyed girl from a mining town
writing adolescent poems of rejection
for something that was never offered
singing on tables and sometimes under them
slipping on a frozen path   the canvas with her portrait
pierced by the stalks of dead chrysanthemums

5

summer loves on the warm concrete promenade
frenzied knickersoff trouserbutton gropings
in the 78 r.p.m. recordplaying frontroom

6

shadowed circle under a summer oaktree at noon
familiar browncheck dress raised high
seeing the strong brown body full for the first time
down the lane past the little yellow house
confident hands guiding me into you
melting elastic beautiful unfamiliar
afterwards sensible scrubbing at dampmarks
hurrying home so your parents won't know

7

O that summer of lightblue eyes and strong brown hands
reflected in black glass café tables
brown El Greco feet running down alleyways of trees
in the Botanical Gardens
home to love summer rain happy down our faces
tasting the rain on your laughing mouth
pink gums above your littlegirl milkteeth
spending our summer wages getting pissed on Fridays
over the iron railway footbridge
kissing goodnight at the end of the semidetached avenue
so your father won't see us
hiding like mice down backstreets when his big black car goes
    past

8

trying to paint
the Pasmore morning world
of City allotments
striped huts abstract against beanpoles
curling tendrils of branches into mist
patterns of green leaves against conservatory windows
zebrastriped trafficsign city
red triangles
grey distances against the bright trafficlights

9

the library for
Eliot Pound the enchanted islands
Kafka   Auden   MacNeice
Sydney Keyes dead before the foreign gate

and for
the beautiful blonde librarian

144

round blue eyes   pale face   child's mouth
full fleecy pinksweatered body
round thighs
watched
across afternoon tenniscourts
across morning bookshelves

10

coming back
to our café
black-and-white-tile floor
still the frothiest coffee north of Sorrento
not
the afternoon hangout for the Grammarschool in-crowd
anymore
now
full of babies with red faces
and middleaged mothers
I suddenly realize
were at school with me

11

PRESTON:
rain splattering my glasses
splintering the neonsigns
24   schoolteacher
in a provincial town

12

meeting you
dark noisy club   nomoney dates
home to my flat

remembering
the morning park   the distant railway
the long green caverns in the treefilled square
loving you
in the crowded coffeesmell Kardomah

13

working
as so often
in the noisy blaring fairground
cream-and-red stalls
creampainted rollercoaster against darkblue sky
working
this time with you
brightlycoloured balloons bursting
ROLL 'EM UP   ONE OVER TO WIN   ANY PRIZE YOU LIKE
powderblue nylonfur poodles
against the bright red counter
children crying   runny noses
holidaymakers huddled like sheep under plastic raincoats
from the August rainstorms
coaches revving up in the carpark
ON THE RED THIRTY-THREE   ALL THE THREES THIRTY-THREE
Frankie Laine   Guy Mitchell
loud through the electric nightrides
lights going out running with the heavy shutters
pints with Big Jim and Georgie Lee in the closingtime
    billiardsroom
fishandchip latenight O'Hara's suppers
concrete promenade still warm under our feet
the long walk home
the Townhall clock and the deserted railwaybridge

146

14

bright still-lifes
proud yellow lemons red tomatoes
orange-and-white Penguinbooks
blue-and-white mug
painted in the little buildershut I rented
down a lane
furnished with a settee for loving you
an easel for your proud body bright against the yellow walls
down to the Dole on Fridays
fairground closed for the winter
flat red sun   black posts   white seagulls
held whirling
against the darkening sands

15

now
the alleyways and market-gardens
gone
instead huge supermarkets empty as the winter seashore
long shoppers
circling over bargains like seagulls
greeted only by strangers
in the unfamiliar streets

III

saturday morning, reading the lifestory of Dylan Thomas
aged 19, coffee in a greenflowered mug, smell of red beans
boiling downstairs for Arthur and Carol coming to dinner. my
brother and a new girlfriend coming to share the spare
bedroom. Sue asleep as always in the big brass bed upstairs.
me at the morning desk as always, trying to write something
I've been trying to write since June 3rd, 1970, the day my

mother died. Tony ringing at 7.45 a.m. me rushing out having to see the bankmanager before getting the train but almost unthinkingly stopping to look for a black tie putting it in my briefcase. he met me at the station and told me the news I'd already guessed dark circles round tired eyes. the last time I saw her in hospital two weeks before, I thought what a beautiful woman she'd been. looking old, thin, wrinkled with illness but the fine cheekbones and forehead there as always. hair bobbed dark against the out-of-focus Florida background of 1930 photos. a blue crêpe dress with a matching summercoat. a darkblue dress with coloured circles like Rowntree's pastilles falling into the distance. not for years the fur coat she always wanted. winesilk danceshoes with diamanté heels. all squashed at the back of the fading wardrobe, in a cardboard box a crushed orangeblossom veil. pushed at the back behind the cheap dresses for the Football Club or the Saturdaynight pub. beautiful young mother holding my hand going for a picnic on the sandhills mysterious to jump off like Sahara now bulldozed into concrete carparks. quick laughing crying emotional quick to read telling me proudly she'd read *Ulysses* in three days. once-a-year concerts of Beethoven. Blake's Grand March or selections from Gounod she'd play on the piano for me. Later there was only the drinking club, dirtyjoke comedians, the hideous songs from musicals. her bending over beautiful in the darkness to kiss me coming in from a dance smelling of perfume and gin-and-lime. alone, sad, watching the shadows on the ceiling, then loving her watching the rainbows in her necklace as she leaned over me. middleaged, shortsighted, too much effort to read anymore, loving the children's popsongs but still sometimes listening to Caruso and John McCormack. as the children grew older she surrounded herself by cats ramifying family black grey tabby constantly inbreeding. once I used to write home describing every painting I did, everything I wrote. when did I stop? why? suddenly she no longer knew the reason why I did them, only proud of me for the newspaper articles, the television interviews. her ambition, more than perhaps anything else, made me what I am. by the time my first books were published her sight was too bad for her to read them.

Poem for Liverpool 8

LIVERPOOL 8:
blaze of trumpets from basement recordplayers
loud guitars in the afternoon
knowing every inch of little St Bride St
brightgreen patches of mildew redpurple bricks stained ochre
    plaster
huge hearts names initials kisses painted on backdoors
tiny shop with a lightbulb in the window
Rodney St pavement stretching to infinity
Italian garden by the priest's house
seen through the barred doorway on Catherine St
pavingstones worn smooth for summer feet
St James Rd my first home in Alan's flat
shaken intolerable by Cathedral bells on Sundays
Falkner Sq. Gardens heaped with red leaves to kick in autumn
shuttered yellowgreen with sunlight
noisy with children's laughter in summer
black willows into cold mist
bushes railings pillowed with snow in winter
Gambier Terrace loud Beatle guitars from the first floor
Sam painting beckoning phantoms hiding behind painted words
    bright colours
in the flooded catfilled basement
pigeons disappearing at eyelevel into the mist
hopscotch-figures vomitstains under my morning feet
Granby St bright bazaars for aubergines and coriander
Blackburne House girls laughing at bus-stops in the afternoon
Blackburne Place redbrick Chirico tower rushing back after love at
    dinnertime
drunk jammed in the tiny bar in The Cracke
drunk in the crowded cutglass Philharmonic
drunk in noisy Jukebox O'Connor's
smiling landlord on the doorstep huge in shirtsleeves and braces

LIVERPOOL 8:
now a wasteland
murdered by planners not German bombers
crossed by empty roads
drunken lintels falling architraves
Georgian pediments peeling above toothless windows
no Mrs Boyne laughing in the Saturdaynight Greek chipshop
the tumbledown graveyard under the Cathedral
where we kissed behind willowtrees
bulldozed into tidy gardens
huge tornup roots of trees
pink sandstone from uprooted walls glittering in pale sunlight
no happy dirtyfaced children
littering the sidestreets
only a distant echo of their laughter
across the bonfire fireengine debris.

PART THREE 1957-64

1

warm diagonal red-and-black tiles
fire burning in the deep chimneyplace
whitepainted wooden rockingchair   white walls
big regency-striped settee
winter in the little basement yard outside
her voice singing high piping in the kitchen
Saturdaymorning nowork breakfast
reading the *New Statesman*
flames echoing on the low white ceiling

2

blue-and-white-striped mugs
a small stone with holes in smelling of sulphur

150

we brought home from a beach one day
pueblo-type ashtray from Woolworth's
the sudden apparition, in red,
of the wife of Pierre Bonnard
on the print framed in the alcove
singlebed mattress waiting upright in the tiny wallcupboard
for my hitchhiking friends

3

sharing with you
Bird, Monk or Mingus
Mathis der Maler, Das Lied von der Erde
Little Richard or Muddy Waters for parties
same violin concerto always to go home with
rising upwards beautiful
into the proud cadenza

4

Henry laughing red bearded punning face at parties
climbing the scaffolding on the midnight Cathedral
Don studio floor piled with paint plaster wood
moon landscapes even higher than his paintings
John from America a battered Volkswagen laden with pictures
I met eight years later in a New York bar
Ben from Mayfair exiled to grotty Liverpool
keeping a club for our latenight drunken fantasies

5

Brown   knocking on the 4 a.m. bedroom window
"Psst. It's me,
Brown"
laughing   plaid hitchhiking jacket   full of news
frantic letters for leftbehind poems
or soiled pyjamas

6

Hawkins
ironing his still-drunk trousers to go home to wife and
    motherinlaw
finding an old clown outfit in the wardrobe
enormous   black   red frills and bobbles
bent over the ironingboard
in the hangover morning

7

on a bus
reading Leopardi, the twisted crookback with the winter's
    smile
patient broomflower "upon the shoulder of the arid
    mountain"
seeing
children filing into school
a young man tweedcoated sadly in the yard, On Duty
wondering
how many exiles to the land of concrete lampposts
the drums and trumpets of success
fading in their ears?

8

still
seeing you on a winter beach
bent forward double from the waist
red jacket black trousers like a wooden soldier
nose tip-tilted
inspecting the sound of barnacles on a lonely post

9

Aldermaston dogs scowling through wire at happy marchers
banners black-and-white against Falcon Field
proud trumpet breaking out over the marching drums
the uphill road   tired legs   feet sore
Joyce and I with the huge wurst sausage
we took every year to eat at roadsides
thrown into horseboxes by grinning policemen on demos

10

now
beginning the time of the infidelities
Carol proud breasts warm everopen mouth
Gail who seduced me in the afternoon newstheatre
Pat
my first schoolgirl love
eating buns on the afternoon ferryboat
carving our names in soft red sandstone
one time encased in plaster
from neck to middle   still feeling your warm body through it
clear blue eyes   darkbrown hair
loving you
even when finding your phonenumber
in someone else's poem

11

seeing
my first Yves Klein
blue universes in a tiny artgallery
lumpen Paolozzi monsters
Newman horizonlight
serene dark Rothko
Robbie the Robot
making "today's homes
so different, so appealing"

12

DEATH OF A BIRD IN THE CITY
screaming white splattered against windscreen
crucified on a nightdoor
black words running
lost girl giving you dead flowers
last night's blood on tomorrow's pavement
smells of icecream and antiseptic hospitals
poems sweets comics foodpackets
sweet little Chuck Berry schoolgirls
goalposts chalked on greybrick walls
"The Night, Beware of that dark door"
dying among bunches of nightblack flowers
painted screaming unheard in the tarmac city

13

in Philip's photograph
your hair
grown from the littleboy cut now
backcombed round
on a tube train

face and body brown
from the everyday sunbathing whitewashed backyard
dark hair longer still
in another photograph

at the bar
in our favourite club
loving
but not making love

14

painting huge canvases of Piccadilly
Guinness Clock MOTHER'S PRIDE
bright garden   yellow flowers   grey buildings
huge hoardings for eggs or cornflakes
DAFFODILS ARE NOT REAL
scrawled defiantly across the middle
or
at jinglebells Bing Crosby brass band Christmas
Dreaming Of
her pale secret face
behind the cardboard Santaclaus and cutout reindeer

15

moving from Falkner Sq.
thrown out finally after so many times
after the first party
back from our last fairground summer
laughing friends pushing the settee on its castors
round the Square
brave new home
in a Canning St attic

IV

I suppose he was a bit of a failure, really. at least in most
people's eyes. he ended his working life earning a week what I
can earn in a night. my mother was always on at him about
money. he'd been a bandleader, a social worker, a jolly uncle
in a holiday camp, a dancing instructor. yet he ended his life
as a miserably underpaid Civil Service clerk in an Army camp
near a small seaside town. he'd written a play, he'd produced
plays, he'd run a magazine written by unemployed workers
during the Depression, he'd worked tirelessly to help other
people. yet because he couldn't really help himself we none of

us ever really admitted what we felt about him. it's hard to believe dead people are really dead. the waxwork-yellow face, the purple-tinged ears in the Chapel of Rest wasn't him. the black hair just tinged with grey was a cleverly fitted wig. there were Alexandra roses growing up the redbrick hospital wall outside. my childhood was a border zone where skirmishes, rocket-attacks, dogfights took place daily. no prisoners taken. "look what your mother's done" "did you hear what your father said". a lonely observer, fired on by both sides at once. when the children grew up and they withdrew behind their own lives it was too late for him to stop. he used to complain incessantly, often to himself, shuffling about in the kitchen or the garden, a Cassandra in a shabby blue suit, a Jeremiah with no tribe to listen, a shepherd-boy constantly muttering "wolf", a forgotten Coriolanus in voluntary exile. still a handsome man even into his sixties, black sleekback 1930s hair always chatting up the prettiest girl at the party. after he died we found a Last Will and Testament amongst his things. the name and address and date were filled in. the rest was left blank.

Poem for Summer 1967

I think perhaps the thing I've envied most
is my aunts' easy tears at funerals
crying for someone they hardly knew and hadn't seen for years
I can't cry for anyone
not really
tears come readily
at the thought of justice or injustice
when they came and put out our bonfire when I was a child
reading Nicola Sacco's last letter
seeing the triumphant crowd bearing banners into the distance
invading tanks and flowers on bloodstained pavements

heard on the noisy foreign radio
not you dying
but the stupid cheap chords of hymns at funerals
brought the tears to my eyes

Scott McKenzie singing "San Francisco"
nostalgic now further away than The White Cliffs of Dover
long soft body in her husband's bed
walking to the bank in the nextday hangover rain
crowded noisy party
Tony and I picking nasturtiums for our hair
in the darksmelling summer garden
faraway summer gone for ever
thunderclouds massing   mist on trees   flooded fields through
     hedges

Canning Street polished flooboards home
sideboard elaborate   brickwashed wall above brass fireplace
bedroom collaged with posters to hide where the rain came in
black cat jumping through skylight on to the bed
polish worn away by so many footsteps
so many different faces on the pillow
painting bright salads
meat oozing red electric in the neonlight
tiny universes of creamcakes
clean white canvas waiting ambiguous
Allen singing washing the morning dishes
Bob Creeley laughing at the cardboard I put in my shoes to keep the
     rain out
Sunday morning sunfilled Albert Dock with Jonathan

Kissing warm snuggled like childbed
Kissing autumn eyes welling up in the darkened hallway
Kissing away from your best friend under every secret streetlamp

flat now empty
Joyce two streets away room with dried rushes and butterflies

laths fractured sticking through falling plaster

wet paper flapping
rain dripping monotonous
broken-tiled steps to the peeling doorway.

PART FOUR SUMMER 1970

1

moving
once again
strange new worlds of limegreen carpet
cat not knowing where to sleep unfamiliar
doors banging at night apprehensive
downstairs every morning to the windowdesk
schoolgirls laughing beautiful past at 3.45 p.m. daily
blue-and-white dishes
in the evening kitchen

2

Rites of Spring
celebrated in a bluecarpeted room
looking on to the treefilled square
grey spring sky tangled in my fingers with your blonde hair
running my mouth down your warm wet body
the night we had to climb a ladder to your bedroom

3

wind moving high in the summer trees
blowing away the wasp that's near my hand
a tiny yellowgreen insect walking across the blue lines of this
    paper
poppies in the tall grass
camomile and dead nettles swaying
farmgate open
fields of rye rippling in waves
smell of tar from the newlaid road
bright yellow light behind my closed eyes
last year's leaves blowing in the sunlight

4

you
the Yorkshire Poacher
singing over metal nests
two buttering happy
for breakfast
smelling the toasthaze drifting
between the cooker and the door

5

purple loosestrife at the edge of the bay
sea flat grey into the distance
early blackberry flowering along the marshes
tiny troutbeck streams struggling through boulders
soft green hills divided by blackstone walls

warm young body under crimson sweater
patched blue jeans you washed specially for today
wind blowing towards us from the dark mills at the end of
    streets

warm mouth warm kisses cold hands cold wind
on the station platform

eating Chinese food afterwards waterchestnut crunching in
    my mouth
remembering crisp white teeth
still feeling your soft body against my chest under my arm
eyes wide amazed at the newness of things
alone on your bike in the 3 a.m. newspaper streets
holding my hand on a summer afternoon
writing poems on your examination papers

flocks of wild geese moving across the lake
loving you in frozen silences of fern and rhododendron
the pathway by the water alive with baby frogs
sharing your wonder at the tiny life jumping to escape
from your cupped hands

6

NORWAY:
parked in the middle of the most beautiful landscape in the
    world
a green-and-red van with SPORTY FORD painted on it
clear viridian depths of cold rivers
waterfalls veiling the sides of granite mountains
last year's snow unmelted   their sides blotting into the mist
laughing blonde girls picking brightpink flowers
old man waiting between the clock and the bed
white birdwings against green fields
small boats lapping at the fiord's edge
unwanted painting
left in the snow outside the painter's cottage

7

you
dreaming of being a salmon
in a lake of crystal water
the scales and dripping waterbeads
changing into a princess's garments
tightfitting hat crusted with rubies and diamonds
trapped by wicked gnomes
in the long grass
across the field
on the way to find the treasure
in the secret garden

8

your familiar voice
on the telephone
happy to type the poems I write for other people
happy to hold the body I give to other people
welcoming me warm into you
happy to make our onenight home in other people's
    bedrooms

9

rust-red rowanberries
against the rustred roof
of an old barn
inside the warmsmelling hay stacked into darkness
scrambling through tiny streams
clear to the marble fragments on the bottom
ferns higher than your head
dead goose crucified on a bright green cowfield
sudden blood   ribcage   white feathers scattered
small dog jumping for the wildflowers in my hand
a cowman shouting and whistling

across the valley
evening falling
only a trout jumping to break the yellowgreen silence

10

you
in the foreground
farmyard
feeding the ducks
and ducklings
hens and chickens
3 white geese
about your feet

11

living in all my London homes
from home
brokenbacked bedsettee   tiny bed in Ted's spare room
big basement bed in Windmill Hill
arguing with Christopher in a pub
trying to purify the dialectician of the tribe
afternoon wine in Bernard's shop
summer haunted by breasts and minithighs
remembered eyes among rush-hour faces

12

Hampstead   aeroplane garden morning
6 a.m. pale gold bedroom daylight
curtains of honeysuckle and wistaria
darkgreen figleaves
modestly concealing the sky
delicate pink light through climbing roses
morning birdsong   the noise of beginning traffic

pears falling soundlessly from heavy branches
Sunday kites high in the clear air
trees   grass   lakes laid out neatly for inspection

13

you
as Little Nemo
across the magic bridge to Slumberland
curled up sleeping on a bedsettee
in the Palace of King Morpheus

the Girl from Porlock
calling me downstairs from writing this poem
to watch you laughing lying back
in our new bathroom
house full of treasures
you display proudly from the market every Saturday

14

along the churchyard
rhododendron   magnolia
distant bell
path I walked with her as a child
to her mother's grave
dead redandwhite flowers
lashed by the rain as I write

15

after the empty years between
suddenly given
the literary
lion's share
but who

to share it with?
the lion sleeps
confused, exhausted.
the dark outside echoes to his cries.

Rhyl Sands
AH '86

HAIKU

HAIKU

for Francesca,
dark lady of winter nights
and midsummer mornings.

leaves fall from the privet-trees in the Autumn backyard
— I think of you

This morning,
throwing out last night's beer,
I gave a party for the birds.

for Elizabeth

morning:
your red nylon mac
blown like a poppy across Hardman St.

for Penny Tweedie

Opening my notebook to summer meadowsweet
In the winter wood.

166

for Ted Joans

I'm dreaming . . .

darkness fallen everywhere:
black santaclaus
coming down
white chimneys.

Bones wait white for the paintbrush:
February snow falls past the window.

Spring in London:
the first alcoholics
blossoming in Euston Square.

Remembered images of you flash past:
Clumps of poppies seen from trains.

Hillsides veiled with fern
Foxgloves last seen with you
A hundred miles away.

1926:
blind ponies
kick their heels
in summer fields
by idle pitheads.

today it is a yellow river
no moon
no drunk poets drowning.

Seagulls
sing the sunset
samphire on seacliffs
echo your footsteps.

A·H. 86

CITY HEDGES

Morning Song

Of meat and flowers I sing
Butchers and gardeners:

When aware of the body's process
The long journey into red night
The unfamiliar pounding that may cease at any moment
Drift off into the night full of sounds
Ticklings and murmurs, whispers and gurglings

When my mouth
Open against the open world of you
Into the darkness of rosepetals
Continents against white continents
Shudder in perspective

When the curtains are drawn
And you blossom into morning
Eyes unveiled from sleep flower-beds thrown back
White lilies against your hair's vine-leaves
I will rise and moisten the warm wet soil
to perfection:

Of meat and flowers I sing
Butchers and gardeners:
Songs thrown bleeding onto counters
Reaching up to the sun through city backyards.

Wartime

I   Hostage

(*in memoriam Ulrike Meinhof*)

Urban Guerrilla
you burst into me
machinegunned
the old poems
stationed at the door
for just such a contingency
made off
with my heart
in the getaway car
despite
a desperate chase
by police in armoured cars
held it to ransom
demanding
nothing less than total involvement.

That night
a bloodless revolution
statues of the old regime
toppled in the streets
victory-fires
lit on every hillside.

Now,
in the final shootout
you fight on alone
at the window of the blazing house
I a voluntary hostage
bewildered
listen to the howl
of approaching squad-cars
taste
the stench of gas-grenades

as the masked militiamen
burst
into the room
wonder
if I'll miss you.

2   Regime

Torn posters flap
wind howls through
rusting hustings
no fate is known
for those deposed
brave new politicians
govern the bedroom
undisturbed by the sound
of distant firing-squads.

3   Truce

After the bitter end of war
and tired troops return
wounded sunbathe
hospital-blue on balconies
retreat
my undefeated lover

starshells will wake us
mysterious armies
regroup by night
between our separate bodies
tomorrow
the dawn attack
the blood-filled trenches
worlds locked again
in loving combat.

172

The Dance of Death

autumn to winter:
willowherb turns indigo
against the orange of its going
bonfires in backyards
hold the fitful dusk at bay
flushed children's faces
candles in pumpkins
strains of the "Dies Irae" heard in the distance.

Dancing figures against the fading skyline
bony feet through withered leaves
leaping singing flapping like stormclouds
Death the Magician
conjuring darkness out of daylight
Death and the Lovers
crouching behind the settee peering through the curtains
Death and the Maiden
cold phalanxes of fingers over goosepimpled flesh
probing the warm and secret places
". . . there will now follow a party political broadcast
on behalf of Death . . . this programme will be shown
on all channels . . ."
Death the Politician
polished white face carefully sipping water
adjusting his fireside manner
DEATH RULES OK
scrawled on a wall outside the football stadium
Death the Terrorist Death the Avenger
O there is no hiding from the secret bomber
the parcel left unnoticed in the crowded discothèque
Death the Trafficwarden Death the Controller
bodies spilling everywhere
trainsmash or planecrash
carbrakes on tarmac
Death and the Soldier
familiar companion

riding a troop-carrier in camouflage gravecloths
Death and the Boatman
steering the October ferry to Eridanus
Death the Popsinger –
obscene spangled bony limbs gyrating –
Death and the Drunkard
grinning behind the barmaid's smile
Death and the Junkie
kindly refilling the hypodermic
Death and the Priest
mocking laughter from behind the altar
sly white face behind the confessional
Death and the Schoolgirl
cold hand up her gymslip in the autumn park
Death and the Farmer
following the furrow seed falling barren
Death in the Supermarket,
Corner-shop, Greengrocers',
Dance-hall and Waiting-room,
Alehouse and News-stand,
Housewife and Bunnygirl
join in the sarabande
hold hands and dance, dance
as the lightnings whirl
dance, dance, dance to the darkness . . .

eve,
and the Michaelmas moon
rise in the firtrees
last strains of music
heard from the deadlands
November dreams
lost amongst stormclouds.

Annabel

Annabel
can't tell
home
before dark
afternoon kisses
still warm
on your lips
rain drips
from privet leaves
in city gardens

Annabel
can't say
can't stay
home before
dark
eyes
bright
through the
rainwet
streets.

For the Girl from the Green Cabaret

(*for Sue Jackson*)

green girl
didn't grow up
don't grow up
stay like the sea
for me
every wave different
always the same
green girl

eat up the buttercups
shamed by your hair
remember what's good for you
green girl

green girl
cry rainstorms
dry your eyes with strawberry-leaves
laugh forests
at noon
sing rivers headlands islands for me
green girl

dream
girl
seen
at first light
flowers
in the night
stay
for me
green
girl.

Galactic Lovepoem Two

(*for Frances*)

Universes
away from you
light-years
from your sleeping back
spindrift of stars between us

after
sharing water
in the yellow desert of the bedroom
dreams
filled with insect-men
warm giants their heads made of animals
counting electric sheep
doors that talk back to you
vortices of time
torn by the alarm-clock

nebulae
in your waking eyes
time-warp
of your morning kiss
this poem for you
through the grey barricades
of daylight.

Metropolis

(for David Gascoyne)

1

gravelponds along long lines
fruit-trees heavy in the autumn sunlight
disturbed only by the falling brickdust
and the distant roar of engines in the morning air.

blackberries glinting in the sunlight
poised against the sky   toppling into enormous pits
hayfields   troutstreams   drystone walls
falling   tumbling   rolling before the gleaming blades
squashed hedgehogs dying owls rabbits screaming
grass and tiny bodies tangled in the clay
before the march of giant earthmovers.

O stars trees ponds
tornup roots of farmhouses
gape into the mist
allnight roar of a thousand cementmixers
acetylene lights flooding the sky.

2

apocalypsis of weirs foaming into polluted canals
endless landscape of factoryfields
chimneys belching dark into the distance
all roads home gleaming far away silver seen briefly through
    the drifting clouds.
vast reactors megatheriums of pylons
tangled webs of cables blotting out the light
save for bright sodium-lights above the rushing expressways
flyover   cloverleaf   underpass
one way only   every which way
roadways layered up into the darkness.

3

concrete empty electric hallways
echoing with the sound of Muzak
shopfronts still boarded   shuttering still on the pillars
scaffolding everywhere through the haze
glass towers into the sky
acres of polished tables   boardroom carpet
empty halls of computers and filing cabinets.

endless escalators   vistas of plump thighs
nylon curved crammed tight with bursting flesh
tight glimpsed whitecotton secrets
soft female smell in the secret darkness
nerveless fingers immobile on trains
touching the warm imagined places
178

vistas of pink nipples haloed through delicate lace
disappearing out of the corners of the eyes.

NIGHT   The neon landscape
the soft purr of skysigns switching on at evening
like the roosting of longdead pigeons
nightlong litany of hammers and rockdrills
green light flickering from the wall-to-wall telescreens.

4

huge bridges   majestic arches
spanning the longdead beds of rivers
dried pramwheels   rusty cans   bones of dead animals
stagnant pools rainbowed with oil
where fishes once swarmed.

limitless vistas of bungalows and tower-flats
behind the highways
obscured constantly by the gathering darkness
ceaseless flashing of commutercars under the yellow lights
gaping mouths of endless tunnels
gleaming silver trains swish and rattle into blackness
old videotapes of trees played rushingly past the empty
    windows
stereo birdsong through the airconditioned silence.

Scenes from the Permissive Society

1   There were no survivors from the dawn raid . . .

(for Richard Hill)

Soldiers of love:
returning at dawn
shock-troops
in the sex-war
dropped
2 doors away
no prisoners taken
cyanide button sewn onto lapel
excuses timed
with a self-destruct mechanism
activated
at the first sign of tears.

2   Poem to be printed on a pair of paper panties

Throw these away in the morning
Like the things we said last night
Words that go bump in the darkness
Crumpled and stained in the light

Promises made with our bodies
Dropped in the bin by the day
Look for the signs of our loving
Carefully hide them away

Straighten the folds in the bedclothes
Smooth out the pillow we shared
Tidied away in the corner
Along with our last lying words.

3

I want a love
as intimate as feminine deodorant
As easily disposed of
as paper underwear
As fresh as
the last slice of sliced bread
As instant as
flavour-rich coffee granules
As necessary as
money
Available
on demand
A love
as glossy
double-spread
full-colour
full-frontal
as a Bunny-girl
(and the only key
belongs to me)

I want a
Number One
Smooth creamy
Hi-speed
Cross-your-Heart
Getaway
Cool as a
Cosy-Glo
Fingertip control
Throwaway
Here today
Never pay
Any way
love.

Dreamsong

Astronaut
of your inner spaces
caught
in the time-warp
of your body
instruments
refusing to register
lost
in the darkness
of your star-spaces
entropy
defeated
by our loving

parallel
universes
lost
in the future
breath of starlight
on our faces
one second away
from supernova
wait
for the sound
of city morning.

Morning

Jars of you
remind
in the morning bathroom
Face Saving Lotion
face-saving motions,
face-saving motions,

crying in the late-night restaurant where we talk instead of
    home
inviting someone back so we can't face each other
something to fill the gap after the telly stops
something to replace the tooknown records on the turntable
unsurmountable barriers of words
turn us like strangers
spaces huge as kingdoms lie between us
in the onceloved bed.

Out of the Railway Wardrobe

(for Rob Conybeare)

Out of the wardrobe. Out of the darkness. Out of the railway
distance. Behind the suits carefully preserved in mothballs for
the next wedding funeral divorce or christening the seats of
the trousers gleaming grey-striped or navy-blue in the faint
light from the end of the tunnel. The tunnel whose sooty-
smelling breath still holds the memory of long-dead steam-
trains. Chugging over points, the blackened sandstone walls
stretching up to the light. Regular rows of strip-lights against
the walls and clumps of willowherb growing in crevices far
above. Behind the slightly faded wine-coloured evening
dress, the wine-coloured satin dance shoes with diamanté
heels, the black afternoon frock with the pattern of tea roses,
the overhead gantries meet the rails at the precise point of
infinity. Out of the warm musty darkness the childhood
slightly scented smell of fur-coats against your nose tickling
you as you breathe in eyes accustomed to the rustling dark the
line of light round the not-quite-closed door as the sound of
metal wheels accelerating across level-crossings grows nearer
and nearer.
    Out into broad daylight your unexpected city faces. Red
marsupial stranger poems clutched warm in the little pouch.
    Out of the wardrobe out of the junction boxes out of the
serge and mothballs the silk and fur out of the sound of

whistles and platform-trolleys. Out of the wardrobe . . .
wardrobe of dreams wardrobe of desires . . . wardrobe of
upholstery smelling of tobacco-smoke . . . wardrobe of the
emptiness of stations wardrobe of memories . . . wardrobe of
discarded female underwear . . . wardrobe of darkness . . .
wardrobe where farewells hang in the glass and cast-iron
roof . . . wardrobe of broken-down patent-leather
tango-time dance-pumps . . . wardrobe with hidden illicit
dusty books on top wardrobe of perspectives wardrobe of
forgotten encounters . . . wardrobe of crashed carriages
splintered sleepers the crumpled metal rusting in summer
rain . . .wardrobe of cheap hotel-rooms of stains on un-
welcoming sheets . . . wardrobe of immobility wardrobe of
rushing autumn landscapes past windows . . . wardrobe of
old-fashioned tennis-racquets and withered rubber bathing-
hats . . . wardrobe where one gossamer floats in the railway
carriage sunlight wardrobe where one pigeon limps along the
platform . . . wardrobe where dreams lie wrapped in tissue-
paper like faded orange-blossom . . . wardrobe where
dreams wait endlessly outside Crewe Station . . . wardrobe
where dreams hang crumpled their buttons missing . . . out
into daylight where dreams float away on the wind tinged
with petrol fumes . . . out into bright afternoon red
marsupial stranger lost in a wilderness of concrete flyovers.

Citysong

angel
dark angel
constant as seasons
infrequent as words
old rainbow midnight
remembered at dawn
breath of wings
on the morning pillow

184

walking
with dreams in your eyes
fragments of lost conversations
on your lips

Red
Queen of my heart
locked
in the Tower
your willing victim
rivers of faces
not hearing my cries

barges
tug at the tides
helpless I drown
warehouse and Ionic column
down
before my eyes

fireweed
on demolition sites
butterfly
beneath the breaker's hammer
sing for me

Red
Queen
of my heart
mistress of my city
lady of the river
you give me

rainbows
riversides
mountains

I give you

fragments of broken dreams
bustickets
torn snapshots

You send me
anthems
psalms
symphonies

I send you
stammered words
shared bedtime-stories
failed songs
trailing away

night into day . . .

waking
with the key to the woods
black cat lost
in pink-and-white flowers

night into day
Sunday churches penetrate the sky
July fifes and drums
in the William-and-Mary streets

night into day
meeting at morning
leaving at evening

night into day
soft weeds sway
in the river's fastness

night into day
down into darkness
drowning in sunlight

186

lady
O lady
day into midnight

last breath
on the morning pillow

silent words

forgotten seasons

angel

dark angel

sudden wings
as the clouds
close about us.

The Triumph of Death

"Thunder in the dark at Adrian Henri's . . ."

1

birdsong
dropping into space between the sodium-lights
footsteps echo on the wet yellow pavement
down the hill lights of the unknown hometown
bright across the river

First faint chords drift in from the orchestra
woodwinds high in the air
light from the evening sun catching the river
dockyards at the end of the street
flicker with the first smudges of flame

sudden skull-head peering from round the street-corner
seen for a moment from the top of the street
shopping-bag in hand
white beckoning skeleton hand unnoticed behind the parked
　　cars
darkling sky clouding the silver water

2

Fanfare of French Horns:
cars pile relentless into each other at trafficlights
grinning skeletal policemen
ride ambulances over pedestrians
klaxon-horns blaring

MUSIC FULL UP:
strings brass timpani
hoarse screams of owls from parks
despairing wail of sirens from sinking ferryboats
roar of exploding oil-tanks
walls of flame round abandoned tankers
figures of men broken on wheels against the lurid sky

high
above
squadron upon squadron
of dark figures
wheel triumphantly
row derisively amongst the carnage
salmon leap despairingly from the boiling waters

3

images from the haunted screen:

in the deserted cinema
a trapped usherette

188

smashes shattering the waxen mask
grinning hideous face beneath
football-crowds melting like waxworks
faces running marble eyeballs fallen from sockets
rooftops at crazy angles
dark figure in at the bedroom window
classrooms burst into flame
a skeleton exposes his rotting pelvis
to the helpless gaze of a class of schoolgirls
4

typists   shopgirls   errandboys
scream hopelessly
run towards ornamental gardens
from the falling buildings
white mocking figures insolently riding the debris
neat gardens in St James's Cemetery
torn apart
wreathed and cellophaned flowers tumbled aside
as gravecloths burst into the light
white blinking stumbling figures
queue at the gravemouths

black crows perch on the remains of department stores
dying seagulls splattered helpless against the sky
vultures wait on the Cathedral tower
busloads of darkrobed skeleton figures
raping laughing dancing singing
a revolving door spins unheeded
the hotel lounge littered with corpses

gibbets long as vermin-poles down the middle of streets
mocking roar of music behind the explosions
thunder in the dark
light only from the burning earth
dark   dark   dark
white bony mocking faces everywhere

5

And you beside me, my morning girl of the shadows
the inscrutable nurse always at the morning bedside
white breasts sprouting naked beneath your black cloak
head thrown back swirls of rivermist in your hair
take me fold me forever in your warm darkness
suck the cold life from my willing veins
lost in a final dark embrace

black barge straining waiting at the riverbank.

Annunciation

(*in memoriam Dmitri Shostakovich*)

". . . till London be a city of palm-trees"
Christopher Smart, *Jubilate Agno*

Yes,
the prisoners shall sing in their chains
and poets burst forth from snowy prisons
the forests will liberate the badgers
and the rusting barbwire of sandy detention-camps
flower forth with evergreen
dwarf birches reach up high as redwoods
streets shall sing where our brushes have passed
black flags unfurled on every hillside

and
    yes,
the beautiful lady with the head made of flowers
will step out of your dreams into daylight
will step out into the street over the disused barricades
will glide thrugh prisons
will appear in mineshafts
and
yes, the last pit-ponies will see again

190

borstal-boys dance into daylight
entire populations
write poems by the light of blazing labour-exchanges
museums disappear under clouds of butterflies
motorways buried in hydrangeas
factories producing bargain dreams
mansions of flowers
rise
on the remains of tower-blocks

and,
   yes,
through the lanes of
Shropshire Somerset Devon Normandy
where we walked
a thousand paintings shall blossom through the hedgerows
pigs picnicking on the remains of factory-farms
giant cakes stretch away magic to infinity

trees fill the bedrooms
our loving
canopied with balsam and fernleaves
thunderclouds for curtains
our bodies
seen only by the lightnings

the taste of you
always on my lips
the smell of you
always in my morning nostrils

Christmas in January
roses blazing through the snow
summer smell of rosemary
eyes dark as remembered hedges

convent-girls all in their green uniforms
will sing anthems for the Annunciation
of Joy

and,
yes,
those feet
will build
Jerusalem
here
pavilions by Antoni Gaudí
flower in every housing estate

Police-chiefs Politicians Generals Heads of Security
wander unemployed through gutted council-chambers
double agents gleefully reveal their identities
see
the white bodies of soldiers
dancing in city parks
uniforms lying mildewed in flower beds
squirrels play on abandoned troop-carriers
animals wander everywhere
my cat making her morning devotions forever

O Yes
the fox no longer fear the huntsman
nor terrace-house the bulldozer
children safe from nightingales
seals play in the wake of ferry-boats
and schoolgirls make love on the desks of classrooms
for
the Goddess
of Love
is here
The beautiful white lady
at the side of the railway line
beckons from the edge of your dreams
Yes the flower-headed lady is here
and astronauts sing her amongst the nebulae
whales boom in chorus from the depths of the oceans
orchestras of factory-whistles
foghorns hooters
loud from the estuary

192

spraycans write her name
on every underpass
choirs of football-fans
chant her praises
in stadiums everywhere

and
my mother
resurrected
beautiful as a movie-queen
will tango through an endless afternoon of tearooms
diamanté heels aglitter
my father beside her
handsome as Valentino

and
  – yes –
the beautiful pink-bodied Goddess
delicate,
pale as dog-roses,
will take off peacock-winged into the sky
into the pink and yellow iceblue
dawn shading to purple
alive with stars
tiny crescent moon
pale above our city

Yes!
out over the grey haze of railway-sidings flecked with gold
of rushing millstreams and dawn light from factories
statues of horses still shrouded in mist
past our window
bodies warm against the cold panes
past the Cathedrals out over the river
past the airfield past the dockyards
past the windows of lovers
trembling at the lightning playing round pylons
past bedsitters and farmhouses
distant as Icarus

soaring into daylight
over icecapped mountains
green wings spread into pale orange daylight

you
die away
on the still air
a tiny patter of kettledrums
the only signal
of your going.

One Year

1973-74
Liverpool – Totleigh Barton –
Hollywood _ New York City –
Much Wenlock

one year:
my lady of the butterfly-tree
bright lepidoptera halo your head
dark green fritillary, brimstone and tortoiseshell
peacock and mazarine
sing anthems for the dying winter

"home is anywhere inside you
borrowed bedrooms
shared dreams"

one year:
the smell of daffodils
fills my head
springtime to springtime
spring tide to spring tide
pounds at concrete promenades

fat white geese
in muddy farmyards
along canals
pigs in appleblossom
osiers and bitter withy
the phantom drummer through the afternoon streets
last light through bushes
and children's faces over bridges
birds through the aspen-leaves of your body

meeting then leaving
like a rainbow in the night
unremembered kisses
gingerbread heart crumbled in a corner
enigmas of the afternoon
creeping wistaria of suburbs

our life goodbyes
the numbered silences of stations

now the land alive with butterflies
foxgloves in hedges
speedwell in clover
thorns against your sandalled feet
glittering turquoise dragonflies
against the troutbrown river

mudflats over the seawall
and woods for phantom travellers

silvergrey
seedpods of bushes
at the water's edge

summer fading to autumn
dying fireweed
drifting smoke in afternoon hedges
gone with the daylight

"borrowed bedrooms
shared dreams"

Bougainvillaea and hibiscus
bright in the California sunshine
trees from the Palmhouses of Liverpool
in everyone's garden
cries of surfers conga-drums in the afternoon
Malibu sand soft to the horizon
smell of chaparral from canyons
along the burning highway

walking along Sunset
sidewalk warm under my feet

Hollywood Tom
at the teenage prom
in Rodney's Discothèque

strange fruit
zapote cherimoya
witches' treasures of pumpkins in supermarkets

"five minutes to kick-off
and forty-five to salvation
The Reverend Ike tells you what it's like
on your favorite TV station"

poet in Disneyland:
walking round
head full of images
no poem to write
a song without a singer

light fading above the HOLLYWOOD sign
last leaves of our butterfly-tree
torn by the winter rain
frayed heads of palmtrees high above the hills
high electric sound of crickets synthesized with the night

"home is anywhere
inside you"

7th Avenue Valley of Nightmares
sirens tearing my dreams apart
can't get back downtown
for the terrible rain
heaps of straining spurting flesh
out into drenching daylight

remember remember the first of November
picking 2 red leaves in Central Park for you
familiar squirrels hopping a step ahead
loving you on Long Island
fall trees auburn all bright to autumn

back again
to familiar flooded fields
last yellow of birches

bare trees
dropped leaves around their ankles

wet feet on cobblestones
dead chrysanthemums through mist

Christmas-wreaths dying
on suburban front doors

"home is anywhere inside you
neon moonlight
dawn streets"

one year
my lady
one year to tell
words lock together move together
stay apart
inexorably as seasons

waiting at demolished stations
wind from the dead land tearing us apart
two heaps of yellowing bones
sing in the intolerable sunshine

lady
do not ask me
of dry leaves pressed between bodies
dry lips grinning from underground
sing of our one-year chrysalid love
butterfly of all seasons
bright badge pinned against the painted sky

sing
of your body white against green lawns
as the morning sky declares its splendour
pale clouds curdled with blood
light running up the motorway

sing
constellations crowning your head
blossom bursting from branches
gardens painted against the sunset
sing of our seasons
appletree and oaktree
maple and holly

one
frail
butterfly
pale
against the darkening sky
lost among branches
flickers in the darkness.

Evening Song

"I will come to you when the light has gone . . ."

I will come to you when the light has gone
When the sea has wandered far from its shores
And the hedges are drenched in evening
I will come to you when the light is gone

I will come to you when the day has gone
When butterflies disappear in the dark
And the night is alive with tiny wings
I will come to you when the day is gone

I will come to you when the night has come
And morning-glories swell in the darkness
Birds lie wrapped in nests of silence
I will come to you when the night is come

I will love you till the day has come
Trees and fields revealed in morning
Birds awake and sing the sunrise
I will love you till the day is come.

Two Lullabys

1

Here is a poem written on the clouds for you
When white bodies dance in suburban gardens
Accompanied only by the sound of lawnmowers
Champagne pouring into empty swimming-pools
Here is a poem written on the clouds for you

Here is a poem written on the sky for you
On the very last day

When skulls and hummingbirds crowd the beaches like
    deckchairs
Seagulls singing their final requiem
Here is a poem written on the sky for you

Here is a poem written in the air for you
When the flood is over
And pigs are left dangling in the treetops
Valleys overturned and rivers upended
Here is a poem written in the air for you

Here is a poem written on the clouds for you
When the poets are gone and the poems forgotten
When a new earth blooms
And the dying heart pumps a song of welcome
Here is a poem written on the clouds for you.

2

Woken and then lulled by the seagulls
Sleep till the sea-fret rolls by
Turn on your pillow till morning
Back to the opening sky

Sleep though the dreams may come crowding
Like mists across the bay
Night-birds will hover above you
Cry to the echoing day

Sleep though the aeroplanes lull you
Dull through the evening skies
Sleep with the seabirds for guardians
Distances lost in their eyes

Sandpipers wade on the marshes
Curlews awake on the plain
Turn to the cobblestone sunlight
Wake to the morning again.

Two Mornings

1

The little town wakes to the morning
tower four-square to the light
pink gladioli scarlet flowers of runner-beans
pinnate raspberry-leaves
coconut from the weekend fair
desiccating in the sunlight

Pink light through opened rose-leaves
yellow privet through the cottage window
the smell of rosemary from the herb-garden
mixed with last night's smell of you
on my morning fingers.

2

in the soft dawn light
2 sandpipers on white rocks stained with seaweed
bed a riot of empty oystershells
wings white barred with dark brown:
one, red-eyed, anxious, peers at the remains of last night's
    meal
the other, red beak extended,
looks towards the ocean
pink-legged belly full with seed
toward implacable horizons.

A Song for A.E. Housman

I walk the lanes of Wenlock
And dream about the night
Where every leaf is shrivelled
And every berry bright

In Wenlock Town the drink goes down
The laughter flows like wine
In Wenlock Town the leaves are brown
And you're no longer mine

Day turns to night in Wenlock
Laughter to early tears
Down by the hill I follow still
The path we walked this year

Come let it snow on Wenlock
Fall down and cover me
Happy I was in Wenlock
Happy no more I'll be.

A Song for New Year's Day

Dawn drenched into sodden day
pheasant wings whirr into morning
high stones guard the hills
villages quietest under the winter sun
circled yews by rotting iron vaults
dripping to misted afternoon
late light dies on puddles along lanes
with no turnings:
now the season turns
mistletoe stamped underfoot on the bar-room floor
the hills encircle, the valleys enfold
mist tucked between like bedclothes
Christmas-lights down village streets
guard the darkness:
now is the solstice
the shortest of days
raise high the glass against the night
light fading over the hills;
still the tall stones await a winter sacrifice
black hills dark with heather

drink up forget the ghost in the chimney-corner
rattle the lock in the door
the watching and the waiting
dance in their turning
alehouse and graveyard, watcher and walker.

Drinker and dreamer move in their courses
turn with the seasons
drink with the dancers
wait for the new year's slow expiation.

Three Landscapes

1

pledged
by the wild plum-tree
kisses
only a bite away
childhood
silence
alive with gossamers.

2

red earth
stillness
lane shuttered
high
above
the sound of ash trees.

3

Dalmatian dog
spotted
against painted grass
your hair
harvested with sunlight.

Landscape, Ulster

(*for Edna and Michael Longley*)

What
do these fields
conceal?

the sheep graze as elsewhere
first signs of spring in copses
the hills the farmhouses
all normal enough

are there boobytraps
behind every blade of grass?
exploding snowdrops?
assassins lurk in every hedgerow?

only the crows walk fatter along the verges.

Night Storm

pink and white
sudden
pale yellow light
silhouettes of trees

left behind the eyes
as the thunder
tumbles
overhead

you huddle to me
a frightened rabbit
hawkwings of light
seeking you
across the darkened plain.

le Thil, Normandy

Heptonstall Memory

a limerick

In the town of the grey granite tower
With the smell of the balsam in flower
   On that final June day
   When we both went away
You turned as the clock struck the hour.

Song for Yesterday's Girl

(for Dennis Woolf)

Spring.
flowering cherry trees lament for lost loves
city streets echo with forgotten promises
snowdrops burst from the graves of village maidens
drowned for love in the dark pool
badgers turn out their winter beds into the red earth.

Spring,
and alcoholics blossom in city squares
first loves sprout along polluted canals
unmeant goodbyes unanswered letters

lilies-of-the-valley in florists' shops and shaded backyards
remember you with every breath.

Spring, and bitter memories sprout like tulips
melting snow reveals buried indecisions
first rhododendrons blink into sunlight
furze, and first dust of buttercups in the meadow
last daffodils die in forgotten corners.

Spring and your face through every landscape.

Butterfly

(for Carol Ann Duffy)

cry
for the butterfly
in your warm hand
hard light
on the threadbare tapestry of my wings
rainbow dust
left on the loved lines
of your palm

cry
with me
helpless
pinned against
stark white
black writing

sing
of your gift
for your lover
as I fall
flicker against your feet

sing
as I die
caught between intricate syllables
your song
pierce my body
butterfly
flutters
at the foot of the page
tiny rainbow
dies for your song
in the evening sunlight.

Don't Look

Don't look in my eyes, then
look at the dragonflies
glittering   look at the river

Don't listen to my words
listen to the crickets
loud in the hayfield   listen to the water

Don't touch me
don't feel my lips   my body
feel the earth alive with sedges
trefoil valerian   feel the sunlight

My lady,
these things I bring you
don't see   only know
a landscape in your body
a river in my eyes

Epilogue

(for D.H.L.)

Autumn
and leaves swirl at the roadside
splatter on windscreens
summer hopes gone
fears for the dark
the long night ahead
light ebbing to the slow horizon

"Autumn,
The falling fruit,
The long journey,"

Prepare for the dark
O bring it home with you
tuck it into bed
welcome him into your hearth
into your heart
the familiar stranger at the evening fireside

Wind howls in the trees
and toads curl into beds of leaves
night moves into day
moths into velvet
hedges brown with dying willow-herb

Open your door to the dark
the evening snow drift in unheeded
light dies from the sky
gather the stranger close on the pillow

seeds lie buried
safe under hedgerows
gather him to you
O gather him to you

Take the dark stranger
Cold under blankets
Gather O Gather
Alone in the darkness.

Death in the Suburbs

The end of the world will surely come
in Bromley South or Orpington

morning in the suburbs:
sunlight thrown like a blanket
over pink-and-white vistas
villas detached and undetached
islanded with flowering cherry,
stone ravens guard the gateposts
the roof left unguarded,
each man's garden a province unto itself
linked only by birdsong
and the tasteful cooing of doves in hedges
magnolia-petals on deep lawns
little clouds of white and purple round rockeries
frozen veils of appleblossom round every doorway.

the earth
moves
sudden
tiny snowstorms of cherryblossom
a black cat runs apprehensive
flocks of starlings
startle from bushes
slow-growing crescendo
of crashing picture-windows
gardens
uprooted
blown   pinkandwhite   skyhigh
frozen agonies of begonias
held for a moment like a blurred polaroid

lawns flung like carpets
golfclubs   potting-sheds   wheeled shopping-baskets
hurled into orbit

deepfreezes burst open
prepackaged meals spilling everywhere
invitations to whist-drives   coffee-mornings
letters to long-haired sons at campus universities
never to be delivered
pinboards   posters of Che Guevara   stereo systems
continental quilts   rows of neat lettuces
blameless chihuahuas   au pair girls
still wet from dreams of Italian waiters
mothers-in-law   bullfight trophies   sensible wooden toys
whirled helpless in a vortex
rockeries like asteroids
blizzards of appleblossom
against the April sunlight

villa after villa
flickers off like television
birdsounds
blur into the silence
like a vacuum
heaps of white entrails
nestling amid lilies-of-the-valley
ripple like tarmac
gravel chatters   the crazy dance of pavingstones
whole avenues implode
gantries and railway bridges
quiet sidings
engulfed by avalanches of privet and hawthorn
waves of chalk earth flecked with hemlock- and nettle-roots
burying commuter-stations.

far away,
the first distant ripples
flutter dovecots
disturb the pigeons

roosting in oasthouses
weekend cottages
doff their thatch to the sky
mountaintops tumble like cumuli
gales of earth
ravage through ryefields
pylons tremble like seismographs
cries of children
circling like seagulls
echo the distance

a
solitary
picnicker
sitting on a breakwater
above the red, flint-strewn beach
hears the distant thunder
as clifftops crumble
looks up from the light scumbling the silver water
to see the horizon catch fire
showers of small stones
smell of uprooted samphire
the last slice of ham   a packet of biscuits   the small black
    notebook
slip away unseen
as the concrete rears vertical
his ears' last echo
the cries of lost sea-birds
one drifting pink petal
catches the dying sunlight.

Red Card

Right from the off,
straight into your penalty area
a quick one-two and it was all over
bar the shouting. Easy
Easy sang the terraces.

Half-time: I've given you a hundred per cent
and more. Two down, and I've got it all
to do again.

At the end of the day
the lap of honour. Your ribbons
round the Cup. I am
sick as a parrot. I am
over the moon you tell the cameras,
the waiting millions.
Back home I walk
alone.

Hill Park

somewhere
it will always be summer
the gardens "flushed with azaleas"
the park on the hill
still
there
even though
the crumbling pergolas
are burdened with bright berries
though smoke loom from burning leaves
or slow
snowflakes
cushion the colonnades
Yes always the thin summer dress
warm hands   bright flowers
rhododendron japonica
though we come here in wintertime
thinking the story ending
pressed leaves   forgotten letters
pale lemon sunlight
slanting to evening
not knowing the summer ghosts
watching our passing.

Girl Bathing

You step from the bath
smelling of apples, chestnuts, avocados
breath of pine-needles about your feet
Deep Rich Smooth Relaxing
smiling Pomona
a fruit-stall on a frosty morning
your laughing fingers will bring joy
to the waiting millions in the bedroom:

Ladies, Lords and Golden Rings
Ninepenny Geese and Sevenpenny Swans
All in a Paper Peartree

Pollyanna of the bedsitters,
Rebecca of Sunnybrooke Terrace,
still trailing clouds of cucumber and rosemary
you will step out and into the morning
like the sun over winter rooftops.

The Goose Girl

(*for Clare Watson*)

caught blue-handed
by the winter sunset
watching you goose girl
– their shapes still white –
by the pale orange water
arrange a magpie's funeral
– hawthorn and roses –
one pale marbled egg
nestled in your basket.

Two Seasons

early spring:
a brimstone butterfly
imitates
the primroses.

late summer:
bees busy in the balsam
peacocks pose
cabbage-whites drift among thistledown.

Autumn Leaving

1

dead leaves
drift through your words
cold winds
blow between sentences
eddy between paragraphs
wet leaves flat
in the backyard of our love.

I am fed up with you hanging out your words
on the washing-line of my life
my dirty linen for your public

between
between your
wet alleyways your dead
wasteland trees
not growing in the lamplight
dark spaces between the lines
and your words don't tell
how our city is empty and
how for seven years

216

bound to you syllable by syllable
street by street paragraph by paragraph.

I shall no longer wait for the telephone
to tell me the poems you write for others
nor wash your lies from the kitchen floor

our love
as silent as words
as noisy as backyards
as desolate as sentences.

I shall no longer clean this bedroom
other women's words snug beneath your pillow
the bedclothes stiff with adjectives

away from you
here
in this abandoned valley
drifts of dead nouns
drowned verbs
hills spread apart
rich orange-red slopes
brazen to the sky
to the sound of you still
on the tip of my tongue.

I will no longer
Hoover the corners of our life
nor
lie back and let you
bury your words in me

words apart
and only the streetlights between us
waiting these years
between lamplight and morning.

2

Onion in December

an onion in December
layers of words
plump with unshed tears
and stored sunlight
waiting on the shelf
for your winter knife.

3

Spring Ending

and
tomorrow
students
will lay gentle flowers
on the bloodstained pavement
where our relationship died
last night.

4

Full and Frank

At summit conferences
we argue
about custody of the deodorant
and visiting hours for the cat
at weekends. Fair shares
of the wallpaper
and last year's European Cup programme.

A pillowcase
a dusty sugar pig
and two dog-eared cookery books
lurk
on the agenda.
218

Our tears
wait
under Any Other Business.

5

Morning Two

waking
and reaching out for you
in the curtained light
the empty space beside me
throbs the stump of our love
a phantom limb
beneath the bedclothes.

6

Robins

Christmas cards come
addressed to the two of us
I wonder
shall I tear them in half?
send you the robins?
keep the holly?

7

Cenotaph

In this corner
of a foreign girl
I suddenly remember how
the smell of TCP
used to excite me
nightly,
how
we came close and then slept.

Now
at dawn
a bugle sounds
I whisper excuses
and, leaving,
lay a wreath upon the pillow.

"At the going down of the drawers,
And in the morning,
We will remember them."

8

Pressing the wings of butterflies for paper
I write you poems at midnight.
Their small, still, silent voices
Echo my words.

Notes for an Autumn Painting

mist.

crisp leaves against grass.

pale sunrise.

michaelmas daisies by the railway line.

dead willowherb –
tops grey almost to indigo
– leaves burnt to sienna.

dying bracken.

saturated grasslands.

pale orange grass on hillsides, red-purple
amid pale brown fallen leaves.

sky washed by the wind.

green and yellow
confetti
round silver birch trees.

mysterious rich viridian patches
across the vallley.

in the foreground
grass yellowed almost to whiteness

and
a space where

the person who will no longer be in the picture
should be.

From the Loveless Motel

(*i.m. Elvis Presley*)

a lovepoem for America

night
remembered
saxophonelights
of the Williamsburg bridge
Caffè Roma
cannellóni   cappuccíni
bowers
of artificial flowers
across the morning sidewalk

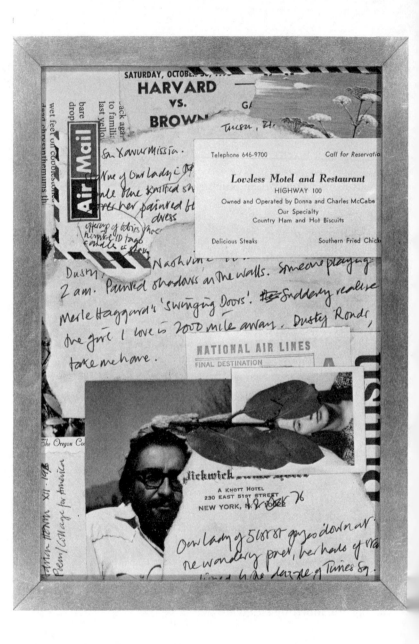

WALK
DON'T WALK

San Gennaro
patient in a dusty shopwindow
gazes down on the little street
waits for his day of triumph

WALK   DON'T WALK

giant puffs of smoke from a huge cigarette
against the sky
                masks
Hallowe'en masks everywhere

GENUINE IMPORTED JUNK $4

lone
black
saxophone-player
outside the church of St Thomas
bright blaze of red-and-white
reared against blue
A train, A A train

WALK

Our Lady
smiles
her 3-D Polaroid
smile

WALK
DON'T WALK
YIELD

curling deltas into brown savannas

EXIT THROUGH THE DOORS WITH THE FLASHING SYMBOLS

electric sound of cicadas
key-limes   mangoes

FOLLOW THE RED SYMBOLS

tiny rainbow lizards
mourning-doves too slow for cats
sandpipers skitter busy across white sand

FOLLOW THE BLUE SYMBOLS

pelicans come up gulping
Alice in a pink-and-white gingerbread wonderland
dimpled brown bringing Budweiser

WALK
DON'T WALK
FOLLOW
FOLLOW

lovebugs die in each other's arms on windshields

THE WORLD'S MOST UNUSUAL DRUGSTORE

                    mermaid show 3rd floor
masks
orange masks

THE FLASHING SYMBOLS

Our Lady of 51st St
her halo of stars
eclipsed by the neon dazzle
of Times Square

WALK

lost in a wilderness of rusting railroad tracks

224

tumbleweed drifting
seeing America from underneath
the peeling underside of flyovers

one more hangover
and a thousand miles to go

YIELD

THE LOVELESS MOTEL

redeye   corngrits
shadowy bellhops
weep
silent tears

Dusty Roads
2 a.m.
painted shadows on the wall
"swingin' doors
a barstool
and a jukebox"
the girl I love
2000 miles away

WALK
DON'T WALK

Dusty Roads, take me home

dark
in his niche
in the ochre desert
S. Francisco
rests
amongst handmade, lace-edged,
satin pillows

FOLLOW THE
smiling hostess like Connie Boswell

FLASHING SYMBOLS

beautiful
barefoot naiads in McDonald's
jumping up then settling like seagulls
wet hair
thin T-shirts over just-formed breasts
("they'd lock you away
for 100 years")

DON'T
WALK

prickly pears
jojoba   manzanita
rusted automobiles
nestling in canyons
snow among aspen-trees
Inspiration Rock
jukebox playing
them sweet country sounds
again

YIELD

turquoise
and one pink
crosses
a tumbleweed
blown against a turquoise-tinselled grave
curled photographs
faded plastic flowers
crêpe-paper stars and stripes
bleaching in the sunlight

FOLLOW

"the white dove
of the desert"

Our Lady
pale blue knitted shawl
over her painted dress
her feet heaped
with offerings

> babies' shoes
> hospital ID tags
> colour photos of servicemen
> little embroidered pillows
> votive images of Robert Kennedy
> tiny silver arms and legs
> one
> child's yellow sock
> names on scraps of yellowed paper

her
gilded halo
caught by candlelight

DON'T
WALK

masks
orange white Hallowe'en bright
saguaros   savannas
red deserts
mapleleaves through mist

FIGHT FIERCELY

invisible 3-D rays
pour from her wounded palms
lost
above the neon signs
above the desert sunlight
from the concrete grotto
from the dusty storefront

227

YIELD

By Grand Central Station
I have sat on commutertrains
and thought of you

WALK

THE FLASHING SYMBOLS

"the loneliest arms
in the world"
on an empty jukebox

my Lady of
The Loveless Motel
be with me and remain with me
now and for always
black-clad
desk-clerk
at the gleaming counter.

Night Carnation

Night carnation,
asleep in the shadows of your hair,
its blood staining the morning pillow.
Outside the snow breathes, patters
on the window. Within
our warmth, the faint persistent scent
insists. Our love
like a carnation in the dark
stains the night air
with its presence.

What Shall We Do with the Drunken Poet?

Thinking of you
On a waterbed
Feeling
Seasick with jealousy.

Football Poem/Goodbye Poem

You never wore
cologne.

Across a Crowded Room

as he glimpsed her
bank-book
it was
cupboard-love
at first sight.

Silvington Songs

(*for Ken and Elspeth Gill*)

1

moonlight
firelight
and snowfall
flicker
behind my eyes
cries
of midnight sheep
from the lambing fields

slow
thoughts
of you
drift
into corners
of my mind
daffodils
through
the snow.

day
slow
tick
of melting snow
in the hedgerows
chaffinch
and rabbit
hop
into greyness
blackbird
sings
in the churchyard
yew tree
for me
wet lambs
gulp free
into daylight
holly
still
decorating the hedges.

lambs kick their heels
in muddy fields
burnt-out candlesticks
of espaliered trees
in cemeteries
dead buddleias
their blackened heads
against the slate grey sky

daffodils
round every grave
in the village churchyard.

2

A Song in April

(another song for A.E.H.)

The buds of April bursting
Into the flowers of May
Await a cold November
Forgotten in the clay

The lambs of April playing
Are due to die in June
The loves of April laughing
Will come to tears too soon

The loves of April blossom
And last a summer long
Come close, for chill October
Will come to end the song

Come close, my love, and tell me
April will never end
That daffodil like gorse-bush
Will last to the year's end

That lambs will dance for ever
And lovers never part;
Come close upon the pillow
And still my restless heart.

3

dawn light
shutters the ceiling
words throb
the millstream spills
into the still air
outside,
snowflakes
powder against huddled daffodils
faded confetti under churchyard yew trees
linked by birdsong

waking,
to memories of midnight sheep
eyes apprehensive in the fitful lamplight
silent Easter madonnas
glittering nativities
golden offerings of heaped straw
lambs,
loosely inhabiting their woolly suits
suck at friendly fingers
outside,
a cock crows twice
denying this birth-day

the mare,
stretched patient on the stable floor
the foal wet and shivering beside her
in the hard electric glare
outside,
yellow bramble-leaves from purple tendrils
against white rhythms of dead branches

now,
as the blue light
brightens on the ceiling
cries of crows dancing their courtship
lamb and foal leap unknowing in the fields

bridegrooms wait at every church-door
mayblossom immanent in the hedgerows

in this bloodstained straw is all our beginning
struggling to rise again uncertain to the light
remember
that harsh midnight
on this beginning day.

United Nations

For years your troops were massing on my borders.
"Joint manoeuvres" you smiled,
handing them their sealed orders.
Eight months ago you ransacked the palace,
took over the radio-station,
broadcast an appeal for calm
to an apprehensive nation.
Too late,
I appreciate
your *realpolitik*:
the treaties, smiles, alliances
a politician's trick.

Wasteland

1

gaunt canals
wet cathedrals   soggy boulevards
leading to no fixed abode
ill winds
blowing from nowhere to nowhere
cracked bells   calling none to worship
stirring dead leaves
round rotting treestumps
. . . *heaps of broken images* . . . wet paper
bikewheels   gas-stoves   dead christmas trees
. . . *lips that would kiss* . . .
pink uprooted sandstone
gleam through the mist
haze of blazing rafters   rooftrees
. . . *eyes not in dreams* . . .
whitewashed walls fall silently
telegraph wires slung pole to pole
across the wasteland

Lady of the Estuary
mudflats   rubbishdumps
. . . *falling falling* . . .
drowned in the sound of distant traffic
my uncompleted graffiti
sprayed on your walls
grey suburbs on a grey day
lead me away from you
echoes of ghostly children's laughter
from forgotten hopscotch pavements.

2

Business is brisk here at the wasteland.
Cars cross the crisscross roads

taking shortcuts to nowhere.
At the coast – they tell us – the seas are rising.

My girlfriend is 21 and says she is doomed
she works in a bar in Rats' Alley
where the dead men snatch handbags.

In the bar,
a skull with a burning cigarette demands her attention
the clock in everyone's face
has stopped.
The face I see in the mirror
is not mine. I drink up and leave.

The pall of smoke grows thicker across the wasteland.
The weather report says "unsettled".
Broken glass like a kingfisher in the sunset.
She will walk home alone, uneasy figures in the darkness.

O dream in vain of roses and butterflies,
the door in the forest,
the dark somnambulist waits at the window.

3

Cruellest Month

We make plans to go away for Easter.
Dream of wet lambs staggering into the Shropshire air
the deep, violet-haunted hedges of Devon
the white cliffs of Normandy, red-stained as the backs of
    Courbet cattle.

Then
decide instead to holiday at home
stock up with decent wines, provisions
loins of pork, legs of veal
broccoli, endives and tomatoes

jostle the refrigerator
the deep-freeze hums its satisfaction.

We settle down,
plan ahead with the TV papers,
the room filled with the petticoat-smell of daffodils.

Outside,
the nightmares howl across the wasteland.

4

The Blues in Rats' Alley

I think we're in Rats' Alley where the dead men lost their
    bones
Think we're in Rats' Alley where the dead men lost their
    bones
Where the vandals smashed the windows and they took the
    telephones.

Tell me, Mrs Porter, what you done to me?
Tell me, Mrs Porter, what you done to me?
Took away your daughter, left me here in misery.

Standing in Rats' Alley where the cats won't walk at night
Yes, I'm standing in Rats' Alley where the cats won't go at
    night
Try to speak your name but you're always out of sight.

Standing on the platform waiting for the train
On the empty platform, trying to see the train
Never heard that whistle, now I'm here in Rats' Alley again.

Take me back, baby, it's you I hate to lose
Hurry back, baby, we don't have time to choose
Take me from this wasteland, don't leave me with these Rats'
    Alley Blues.

5

(*for André Breton*)

these

waste

lands

vague terrains

and the moon

where I wander

indecipherable statues

old boxing-gloves

lonely as

shards of shattered saucers

and the shadow

from the dance floor

a host   a cloud

of

roots that clutch

stirred by

ill winds   lost laughter

down

fall

of the evening lands

blowing from

nowhere

to nowhere.

Moon-Clover

Black-hearted clover
away from our sight
Why do you blossom
only at night?

Why do you bloom
as the moon fills the sky?
Why do you flourish
away from our eye?

Black-hearted moon-clover
shunning the day
Remember the field
where my love and I lay.

An Incident at Longueville

(for John and Ann Willett)

1

It is early afternoon. Late summer sunlight fills the street.
The sound of bells. She waits outside the Café Tellier.
She has been there since the bells in the slate-spired church
last rang. Dark hat, almost like a beret, pulled well
over her eyes. The shadow of the awning of the Café Tellier
falls at an acute angle. She waits with hands in pockets
head down does not see the shadow nor hear the laughter
of the five girls walking arm-in-arm beneath the little railway
     bridge
at the end of the street.

2

Bells again. It is le Quinze Août and the town closed
for holiday. Still she waits head down unseeing.
The laughing girls have long since gone. Baked mud and brick
     walls
reflect the heat. The gravel of the forecourt in front of the Café
     Tellier
stirs beneath her foot. The shadow of the awning has moved,
imperceptibly. The crossing-bell and the heavy breath of an
     approaching
train. The foot turned out towards us taps unconsciously on
     the gravel
to its rhythm.

3

Catching her breath slightly from the uphill walk,
too hot in the thick coat with the fur collar, her
tight shoes resent the cobblestones. She walks into

the Place du Calvaire, then waits in the middle of the little
    street
behind the monument. A child watches, incurious,
from outside his garden gate, blue school smock on despite
    the feast-day.
In the background a tall fir tree overgrown with ivy. The ochre
walls of wood-framed barns. The shadow of the Cross
falls on the brick wall behind it, the arms a shallow angle
to the single band of yellow brick. Its two metal supports are
    shadowed
like a corollary.

4

She stands as before, head down, no longer hearing
or counting the bells. No traffic turns the steep corner
by the Cross. Hands still in pockets, she stares at the base
of the sunbrick wall. She does not see nor think of the frozen
    bronze agony
whose harsh shadow shifts yet again as we watch.
    Lengthening
shadows in a red-tiled kitchen await her return.
Le Quinze Août, Feast of the Assumption, the festive tables
are ready. Soon she will walk out of the Place du Calvaire.
In the dark forest along the valley a white château dreams.

5

She walks away from us down the Rue de Belgique. The
    shadow
outside the Café Tellier has lengthened almost to vertical.
Round the corner by the épicerie trots a white horse,
bridled but not saddled, led by a fat, unsmiling workman,
cigarette and bleus de travail. The man who rides the horse's
    back
is made of flowers.

September Poem

(i.m. Mao Tsetung)

The East wind blew bitter in the night
quiet in the morning
dead chrysanthemums in suburban gardens.

Will the flowers
planted at the graveside
bloom another year?

And will the East wind
blow so fierce again?

Train Windows

1

I think of you
in a blue dawn
tractor against the horizon
garlanded with seagulls
orange sun
across frosted fields.

2

thin snow on the mountains
guillemots on empty beaches
the sea lying placid
white as milk in a blue saucer.

3

woods
dark as your eyes
white birds against flooded fields
red-brown water
lapping round railway lines.

4

dusk streams
and the late cries of sea-birds
last light through trees
blue tents of camps where bugles fall
before the busy dark.

For Our Lady of Darkness

I awake from daydreams to this real night
— James Thomson, "The City of Dreadful Night"

(*for Fritz Leiber*)

1

There is someone in my house.

The step is in pieces and a bookshelf has fallen off
the wall. All night there are hushed sounds
almost drowned in city traffic.

There is someone in my house.

A picture fell yesterday and a window has cracked
mysteriously. Doors slam. The towel
is never where I left it.

There is someone in my house.

The walls whisper. The floorboards creak
to themselves. The telephone will not speak
unless it is spoken to. Who
is there? Why do I
never see you?

There is someone in my house.

2

Treading the porous blue plain
dust raised at every step
bright as cineraria
Murillo children clinging in a doorway
childhood dreamworld of giants and terraces
the words I write at the bedside
run away like milk
the dream you
will not let me remember them
the real you
warm beside me.

At the edge of the dream
where the words fade
she is there
in visible presence
silent
crepuscular
Our Lady of Darkness
the noseless one.

3

I wake to constant pressure. Deadlines
never met. Headlines in every newspaper
proclaim my uncertainties. On the windswept corner
by the Cathedral I finger my guilt
like a rosary. We
wander the empty city. Shuffle
round the grey floorboards
of the Nigerian Social Club. The
nightmare orange of the Gents Toilet resounds
to the splash of ideas. "There's no need
for language" says the man
next to me. Widowed weeds
in disused graveyards. A rat
leaves a stinking skip. Painted barges
locked in grey canals. Arterial trains
stopping everywhere. Stumbling figures
loom red banners through the mist.

What is this city we have come to?

4

in this
interregnum, regency, dormition,
in that
black instant when the world goes down
I walk the silent streets
blind stockings   damaged memories
underpasses like black holes
neon pale as wisps of daylight
pain of endurance. Vast blue plain
stretching uncertain
burnt-out stars   black daffodils
noiseless Golems
noseless
244

mothwings, spidertrails in the darkness
triumphs in the endless night
furtive enigmas
lost moon   black neon
no goodbyes
green sun   black sunset
dark Lady
mother of the shadows
Madonna
of the images
we who are about to wake
salute you.

Spring Poem

"be quiet say nothing
except the street be full of stars"
                    – Pablo Picasso, translated by David Gascoyne

except the canals be full of evening
and our hands full of lamplight
the sky the colour of irises

except the tomorrow sunlight fill the room
pale as your discarded underwear
and the streets be full of the taste of your body

except we open the door in the forest
and step out into the hallway
your eyes a prayer without end in the darkness

except
that the tides of the year will move through the sand
beneath the houses

beneath the plane trees, the bicycles
beneath the cobblestones, the sea
beneath my body,
your body.

Package Poem

the mountains sail O so clear improbable
a painted backdrop from
King Kong

ochre dust
purple morning-glories against dark green leaves
grey-green olive trees   buzz like telegraph poles
crickets and cicadas working 24-hour shifts
HAWAII   RUMBA   BERMUDA   TROPICANA
names that make you think the sun's shining
even when it isn't

conversation by a news-stand
"Ere, Spurs got beat 3-0"
"Where?"
"Look, here."
"I'm going to buy that fucking paper so I can tear it up."

HOLE IN THE WALL: Ye Olden English Bar No. 4
Ye Robin Hood Bar
("chip butties,
cornish pasties")
REAL TEA – NO TEA BAGS
JUST LIKE

sleeping villages perched high on the rocks
weary tourists trudge the Stations
the cemetery highest to heaven

like fretful schoolchildren we grumble
speculate on the inscrutable menu
"Wild Boar's Head"   "Partridge-Sausage"
"Liverpie Sandwich"   "Rice á la Maniera"
chips
appear guilty
under daily aliases
– Potatoes "Dado"

246

Pommes Espagnol –
we bear our own HP Sauce Salad Cream
religiously to every meal. The couple from Gravesend tut,
disapprove "Can't stand
all that rice and stuff", tell
how the Dover Sole turned out to be
squid

la Sirena del Puerto
gazes from the headland
ignores the paella and calamares at her feet
white dust along the lane turning the fir trees to pale filigree
smell of sagebrush and samphire in sunlight
a rainbow lizard
scuttles in the shadows
a tiny train
chugging between lemon-groves

laughing tourists fed from wine-skins
like piglets in a battery

a rich green luxurious palm frond
leans across the garden wall
playfully brushes the faces of an old couple
from Birmingham
"Wants cutting."

"Yes, wants cutting."

patient rows of souvenir donkeys
queue at every streetcorner
their plastic eyes impassive

Lumumbas Cuba Libres
VERY OLD BRANDY 55 ptas a Bottle
MANDY LOVES MIGUEL   ALBERTO Y MABEL
the beach at dusk   mysterious riding-lights

a Bassett-Hound at sunset

parrots and monkeys and small birds
asleep in cages in the dark
stark silhouettes
of palm trees

dogs howl
Echoes of "Qué
Viva España" from every streetcorner
above the buzzing tideless night.

Words Without a Story

(from "Geschichte Ohne Worte": 60 woodcuts by Franz Masereel)

1

In the city we meet. Incurious lightning flickers in the
distance.

2

Almost meeting in the country, you turn away from me.

3

Hand on heart I swear my devotion: you turn from my noisy
streets to your silent arbour.

4

I light candles, monstrances for you: you cast your eyes
downwards.

5

Wise as a shepherd I counsel patience, reason. You touch the
cat rubbing against your leg.

248

6

I speak these words for you, the sunrise spread like a peacock
behind me;

7

I bring gold and precious stones bright as the rising moon;

8

I fall to my knees in supplication; ignoring all these things,
you watch the birds in the garden.

9

Wildly I implore you: you bury your face in a rose.

10

By candlelight I consider other strategies. You hesitate.

11

Beneath the gaze of the servile waiter, you sweep away from
the table.

12

I follow you with bouquets, telegrams. You walk into your
flower garden.

13

I set off ecstasies of fireworks. You cover your eyes.

14

On the steps of the Bourse I juggle bright coins: you pause a moment.

15

I weep in the jungle. You turn, indifferent as a tiger.

16

Distraught I implore you in the city. You step behind a barrier of concrete.

17

Feigning nonchalance, I propose a sophisticated arrangement. The parrot mimes your departure.

18

I am photographed amongst orchids, guinea-fowl, cassowaries. You are unimpressed.

19

I step from my carriage, lamplight gleaming on my well-brushed hat. You are equally unimpressed.

20

In the dismal swamp I step out in rags, touch your dress. You do not notice me.

21

In the farmyard I confront you, tear my clothes away.

22

In the orchard I display myself erect before you. You peep between your hands.

23

At the turn of the stair, I pause, perplexed. You are preoccupied.

24

At the circus I juggle bright balls, turn cartwheels. You permit yourself a smile.

25

Frantic I turn the world upside down, then stand on my head for you. Still you do not react.

26

I bring back rainbows, planets, nebulae, strange interstellar creatures. You seem amused.

27

Emboldened I dance fandangoes, tarantellas. Hired musicians play in the orange-groves.

28

I sing the song I wrote for you, my voice rivals the blackbird's. You cover your ears.

29

Sweat pouring from me, I raise whole officeblocks. You step neatly from the picture.

30

In the midst of starving millions I entreat you. You are remote
as tall factories.

31

My limbs aching, we meet in the midnight churchyard. You
are demure, flirtatious.

32

Where the cross looms at the junction of seven roads you will
not wait for me.

33

By the railway-line I slip my hands boldly beneath your arms.

34

In the alley where the cats howl their love I touch for a moment
the warmth beneath your dress. You slap my hand.

35

From the very flames themselves I cry out to you. You shrug
your shoulders.

36

Where the willows rise urgent as my desire I am bold as the
wind. You touch your breast for a moment.

37

My love is fierce as a tempest. Fish flap in the trees and tritons
play beneath a dark sun. You are estranged again.

38

In the dark wood where the poison mushrooms blow I step out, knife in hand. You call my bluff.

39

I throw away the knife, weep my contrition. A hart appears, magic light streams between his horns. You do not see him.

40

On the steps of the Cathedral I kneel. The bells cannot call you back.

41

Doglike, I crouch in Skid Row. The scent of your petticoats brushes past me.

42

I throw my filthy arms around your dainty feet. You call a policeman.

43

As you kick me aside I think: this is the first time she has touched me.

44

The drunken city flies back at crazy angles. You permit a flutter of your fan as you pass.

45

Reeling I perform a hopeless jig. You do not even see me.

46

Like a depraved mountebank I leap, cavort. There is only a
distant echo of your laughter.

47

I will throw myself into the moonhaunted sea. The laughter of
the drowned echoes your disdain.

48

I step onto the balcony. The traffic roars beneath. Perhaps
now you will listen.

49

As I prepare the rope the black carriage rumbles past. Crows
and the sound of bells fill the sky. You hesitate.

50

In the potter's field the bony hand an inch away from mine,
you slowly turn.

51

The dead themselves crowd to see us as you step towards me,
sudden light in your eyes.

52

Your lips on mine, all earth and heaven forgotten.

53

Impatient you fling your clothes away. They fall like petals
your body pale as sandalwood.

54

Your eyes closed we roll amongst galaxies. I am aware of a distant star.

55

Back on earth I dress myself wearily. Naked and bestial you twine yourself around me.

56

Your eyes your dripping body demand. Clouds fill the sky. I cannot hide the distance in me.

57

Tears fall between your hands. At the window I wait for the rain to stop.

58

You spread yourself before me the white breasts the once-imagined darkness between your thighs. I move away, quietly.

59

As I slip finally from the picture it shows you slumped against the earth. Your tears are bright in the sunrise.

60

Now only
THE END
is between us.

Any Prince to Any Princess

August is coming
and the goose, I'm afraid,
is getting fat.
There have been
no golden eggs for some months now.
Straw has fallen well below market price
despite my frantic spinning
and the sedge is,
as you rightly point out,
withered.

I can't imagine how the pea
got under your mattress. I apologize
humbly. The chambermaid has, of course,
been sacked. As has the frog footman.
I understand that, during my recent fact-finding tour of the
    Golden River,
despite your nightly unavailing efforts,
he remained obstinately
froggish.

I hope that the Three Wishes granted by the General
    Assembly
will go some way towards redressing
this unfortunate recent sequence of events.
The fall in output from the shoe-factory, for example:
no one could have foreseen the work-to-rule
by the National Union of Elves. Not to mention the fact
that the court has been fast asleep
for the last six and a half years.
The matter of the poisoned apple has been taken up
by the Board of Trade: I think I can assure you
the incident will not be
repeated.

I can quite understand, in the circumstances,

your reluctance to let down
your golden tresses. However
I feel I must point out
that the weather isn't getting any better
and I already have a nasty chill
from waiting at the base
of the White Tower. You must see
the absurdity of the situation.
Some of the courtiers are beginning to talk,
not to mention the humble villagers.
It's been three weeks now, and not even
a word.

Princess,
a cold, black wind
howls through our empty palace.
Dead leaves litter the bedchamber;
the mirror on the wall hasn't said a thing
since you left. I can only ask,
bearing all this in mind,
that you think again,

let down your hair,

reconsider.

PENNY ARCADE

I Have Woken This Year

I have woken this year
to the delicate half-light of Devon
to the echoing police sirens of this city
in the innocent white light
of the Cheshire countryside.
And I have woken in her bed in Berlin
in the soft lamplight of dawn on Apo. Paulus -Str.
Woken in a four-poster
huge in a huger room in Cambridge
an old guest
in the Old Guest Room
woken to
the strange brown unexplained stain
on my bedroom ceiling
often with you beside me
our unexplained stains on the brown bedclothes.
I have woken on a train
looking at the breasts of a stranger
pink path across a pale-green cornfeild
woken in a hotel room in Würzburg
stained with the faintest pantie-smell
of the daffodil she gave me in Munich
to day through the skylight above your window
– *daydream believer* –
and the shared roselight of a caravan in Malvern.
Woken in Rotterdam
blood staining the morning sky
poems drifting like gossamers from plane trees
to the grey-brown suck of light
on a Thames houseboat.

Woken in a heap
at the foot of my own
green and unHoovered stairs
and woken (worst
of all) amid the remains
of a small bamboo table
and huge jagged moons of glass
Victorian stuffed birds suddenly exposed
to twentieth-century morning
the telephone buzzing
inexplicably in my ear.
And I have woken to my fiftieth year
two thousand, two hundred and something mornings
my fiftieth year to heaven –

. . . fifty years
and moved across the river
one cobbled hillside exchanged
for another cobbled hillside.
That one/grass between red sandstone/echoed
to the cries of coalmen, bawlies, muffinmen,
steps shining with Cardinal
kids slid on trays
in winter. Here
we sip German wine on the step
in spring sunshine
hosts of golden daffodils
on windowsills/night-time echoes
of riot vans/barbecues in backyards
kids' skateboards
clatter the pavement.
I have woken in this street
to palest winter dreamlight
springlight of children's voices
sunlight through these yellow curtains
the empty pillow of autumn.

I have woken to all these years
all these places,

woken to so many worlds,
how many more summer mornings?

As if in a Dream

"Then would my love for her be ropes of flowers, and night
A black-haired lover on the breasts of day"
    "Black Marigolds", trans. E. Powys Mathers

It is as if in the light of a dream that I see you,
accidentally,
smiling from that doorway.

black marigolds

First Saturday-night feverish flush of kisses
warm vortex of dark irises
lost breathless in the depths of afternoon
dimpled hills hot in this salt oasis
the hollows of your throat smelling of tamarind.

I wake to a metallic buzzing,
a bluebottle trapped in the room,
dozy, aware of your absence,
it circles far above the city streets,
the shattered windows.

One geranium petal
stuck to my green front door
as we leave.

Early October rain
shuffles across the city garden
pattern of first faint light on the window:
in the London basement bed
I warm my hands
at the still summer centre of you.

The wind that has subtracted chimneys
is wiping the slates clean,
blows
your dark-blue spotted dress
showing
cheeky fifties' stockingtops
on the empty promenade.

Silver-pink horizon
rocks imitate sheep. Sheep
imitate rocks. Bushes
huddle like pensioners
round sodden bowling-greens.

Ravenglass sea
lurks in the unseen darkness
like someone behind the childhood door.

I press summer words for you
into notebooks, like flowers.
Find them again
faded as winter.

black marigolds of summer . . .

On the sky above the bed
there are stars like tree-lights,
street-decorations. I reach out, find you,
warm, mysterious, unexpected,
as the childhood rustle of tissue-paper,
unfamiliar woolly shapes in the dark. Your
bodysmell beneath the bedclothes, rich,
elusive as fir trees. The ghosts of loves past,
lovers yet to come, line the mantelpiece,
persistent as Christmas cards. On the carpet
your clothes lie, forgotten as wrapping paper.

Tomorrow the cold, leftover bed served up,
empty as Boxing Day.

Phantom trees
inhabit silent fields:
in the snowfilled dark
ghost telephones ring
in the crevices of the wind.

" . . . drenched in the blood of love"
we confront ourselves
hands   faces   bodies
murderers' masks
in the bedroom mirror.

"I love you as much
as Friday is pig-day" you say
in a letter.
Uncontrollable as words
piglets litter the morning marketplace.

You left behind
among
scrap-heaps, desolate canals,
the concrete underbellies of flyovers,
new streets built over old pavements.

Here the busy river dimples past
brown mirrorbanks
slow suck of wellington fields
the prickling sound of sodden grass
and the brief life of primroses.

Black undersea earth
and tractors turning into spring
beside still lodges

dark obelisk in the abandoned graveyard
filled with daffodils

wallflowers and periwinkles
down the village street.

Eyes dark
above armfuls of midnight daffodils
after Tennyson we lie
on a bed of Daffodil sky.

Singing singing
buttercups and daisies
you walk into the bedroom:
outside a March wind
tears through the the May sky
lilacs and alsatians
blossom in city backyards.

"Some freesias for you
all the way from Birmingham
in a fast white coach"
their smell
a haiku left on my doorstep.

marigolds bloom again
November escapades
crowd the summer afternoon.
Wild strawberries hide
inside the darkness of you
my lips stained with their secret juice.

Warm glow of cornfields
warm brick wall
before the orchard
rapid volleys of birdsong
like mortarfire across the valley
I walk the hillside

under constant surveillance by butterflies.

Now you lie
in the Cheshire sun
with no knickers on
speedwell peer
into the shadows of your thighs
daisies
modestly avert their eyes.

Splashing barefoot through streams
across a Devon lane
laughing in warm summer rain.
The raw umber of Thames mudbanks
sings our departure with the creaking tide.

Extract of Ivy,
Orchid, Green Apple,
Peaches and Almonds,
Lemon and Rosemary,
all the bathtime, bedtime
smells of you

The first soft light of day
fills this sunken garden
with the gentle yellow touch
of autumn. Violet against silver
pigeons bedeck the lawns
against a dream of willows
crowned with stone pineapples
and pale crimson roses.

A hill-fort
holds out against the dark,
drumrolls of cloud
unfurl the last flags of daylight.

black marigolds
in the desert of a long-lost summer.

264

Harbour

(for G. P.)
  – "a place to wander in" –

1

and always
a constant
rainbow
as the northern star   rainbow
stretched across
any estuary
and six swans swimming
where
seven colours burn
as you turn
turn with the air at your back
twin seashells at your ears
with no sounds of ocean
swell of seagulls and the harsh cries of tourists

"once more
to this star"

and also
the little boatlights
harbour of your arms
the darkness of your eyes
reflect the bobbing sea
folded to ourselves far
above the rain   the quayside
constant
as this rainbow constant
fixed
this harbour, estuary,
High Holborn, low pavement
cobblestones along canals
gate of darkness

where white breakwaters are
to meet this
once more
rainbow.

2

from the depths
a shipwreck
nervous swell
of harbour-bell
and the chime of waves

in this dark-
blue world
the long
the endless pilgrimage
to dawn
the nightly sacrament
long vigil to daybreak
kneel at this altar
images distilled
by you – product of tides
and touching, moon and madness – the sweet
deep taste of this harbour
fills the empty world
words lie limp
await a final coming

at last
the carnival departs
skeleton and moon-queen walk the silver streets
last of the sun
shining hibiscus of light
dancers inhabit
the throbbing night.

3

occasions past – this time,
these things – the journeys to take
through white paper
more difficult than mist or mirrors
this bleak sunset
over the gasometers the towerblocks
in some other world
that does not know you
does not own you
the girl
in this white page
with seashells at her ears
is no more you
nor was since she appeared here
this black rainbow
not appear behind her
stark words
against no harbour
– real, remembered –
this page no oily haven
two words
not six swans
this white desert echo the cries of
no seabirds.

4

"and the hue of skin of the figure
was of the perfect whiteness of snow"

and
always to return
to this place
rainbow and rain
and six swans

constant

or other   the folded vision
safe haven   dark harbour
and lights   riding

dancer and drummer
seagull and salt spray
season-song of constellations
black and silver
orange
and pale magenta of willow-herb
starlight of Michaelmas daisies
along embankments
        – "the cluster of low shrubberies
        the slanting of tall eastern trees" –
one white wing spotlit
against the rising night
outside of
ancient calculations
candle-lit nightmare
of empty passageways

lost
dazzled
blinded by
your eyes
        – "the scent of the violet,
        the star-mirroring depths
        of lonely wells" –
eclipse
these constellations
constant
"cold with disuse and forgetfulness"
drifting, helpless
in what white night
carried always
towards this kingdom
hardly glimpsed

sphinx of the ice-floes
lost and drowned   all shipwrecked mariners
before this white altar
dark harbour   pilgrimage
into what new dawn
what fortunate landfall
trawl for words
in what warm seas?

emblems of winter –
    hawthorn and rowan tree
    stooped with berries
    crimson provisions
    against a lichened valley
    bonfires   woodsmoke   the smell
    of wet chrysanthemum leaves
    the hiss of city traffic
– not efface
this time   that place
our footsteps
your face against the streetlights
or summer rain beside canals
the rusty eloquence of the empty pier
or
      once more
this harbour, rainbow
constant
your white coat, pale shell earrings
as the northern star
fixed
proof
against
all armoury
of times, places
body shared with
other faces
on the morning pillow
though
the two foxgloves

in your shadowed hedge
grow
another year
for someone else

constant

not forgotten

proof against dark seasons
– harsh words, tears
  and telephones, cold
  stranger's eyes across the café table,
  these words
  strewn like autumn
  on the foreign pavement –
to return
always
to this place
this sudden
summer rain
fall
always
through these words

rain

rainbow

swans

constant

dark

harbour

as the light

press
of seabell,
seagull

once more

to

this

white

paper, body,
seashell, raincoat,

constant

swell

these eyes
enfold
this universe.

Seaside

1

dawn chorus:

Like angels awaiting some fishy nativity
in the lace-curtain light
hosts, perspectives of seagulls fill the sky
shriek and gibber
I lie like leather in whatever stone you choose to set
their raucous cries fill my head
like the sheeted dead
you stir in your sleep
away from me.

2

Gaily painted pleasure-steamers
ply their trade between us
from my headland I scan, anxiously,
the expected messenger is not
in any of their argosies.

3

The sea has carefully mislaid the beach
beyond our reach. It looks like rain.
Over the boardwalk bridge we trace in vain
your lost shell earring – remembered image
of harbour, swans, and rainbow – gone, perhaps
back to its watery element.

We examine its green brothers in the Shell Shop
and do not find its like. Its lack
as tangible as absent-minded station kisses.
Your eyes as distant, clouded
as the sea in its remote horizon.

4

We sit on the pier and talk of growing old.
A seagull wheels, agelessly. The sea
moves restlessly from right to left. Before
the fishermen cast their lines. Behind, the dodgem-cars
are tuning up. BINGO. SOUVENIRS. The painted shapes
of clouds unreal as candy floss. The distance gapes
wide as the emerald gap beneath the planks,
between our feet.

5

There was, I remember, something about a harbour.
And, yes, a rainbow and – what was it?
Swans, yes, that was it, swans – laughing
we pass unnoticing the window. Our sepia faces
frozen, helpless.

The Business

It's always men who do you wrong
So why not make them pay?
You'll find a friend who'll put you wise
Why give it all away?

The ship girl

The last one was a Dutchman, the one tonight's a Greek
It's just like being married but it only lasts a week
And then it's down the House of Sin to find another one
I wish I could just sail away and no one know I've gone.

O Brothers, tell your sisters
Not to go where I have been
Spending my life with sailormen
Down in the House of Sin.

The massage girl

You'd like to do so many things
Your wife won't understand
Lie down, we'll soothe your cares away
Just leave it in our hands.

The call girl

My grandma walked down Lime Street
And they called her Maggie May
But my name is Michelle
And things are different today.

A contact girl, a contract girl,
With candlelight and wine,
Just dial my number any time
The pleasure will be mine.

The street girl

Upper Parly's cold and wet
It's colder in the Square
I'm here beneath the lamplight
You can always find me there.

When he left me I was six months gone
So what's a girl to do?
I never got my CSEs
All I can do is screw.

It's the oldest game a girl can play
This every woman knows
By day and night, in rain or snow,
The business doesn't close.

In hotel lounge or on the street,
A cabin or a car,
A photo on a glossy page,
You need us: here we are.

Rainbow

Seven Places for Maurice Cockrill

1

Soggy ponies in a New Forest hailstorm
wet almost red bracken. Black line
of cloud to the far horizon, moulting
like cat's fur, sweeping curtains of rain.

Now trees against the sunset, and deer
deep in wet grass and bluebells.
The red mud stiff beneath our feet.

Lyndhurst, Hampshire

2

St Just-in-Roseland: orange lichens on gravestones
dark ramsons massed with white flowers
palm trees campions bluebells primroses
heaped above each other.
Herringbone brick of walls through ivy and young ferns,
berberis and alexanders. Frayed stems of coconut palms.
Grey stone against the brightness of orange-pink azaleas.

St Just, Cornwall

3

Breasts bloom like crocuses in the lunchtime sunlight
underwear blossoms on estates
stern yuccas guard suburban gardens
fishermen sprout beside still lodges
beneath blank hillsides.
In York daffodils flood the walls
and a sweet-voiced girl wears the station sunlight in her hair.

York

4

Faded confetti under churchyard yew trees.
Willow aslant a brook, haunted
by wild rhubarb. One low curved tree-trunk
mirrors the water. Yarrow and moon-daisies.
Yellow monkey-flowers against pink rocks
in the cool viridian shadows. Above our heads
the moor waits, patiently.

Silvington, Shropshire

5

A blue poem
written with a
blue pen
on a morning of
blue hills
calm brick farmhouses
and children's laughter from the other room.

Tattenhall, Cheshire

6

Fête champêtre: ducks in the dusk,
painted butterflies over painted trees darken to autumn,
lost voices whisper in empty drawing-rooms.

ghost dancers flit past shrouded columns
dusty Sèvres trembles to the sound of the *valse*.

green-painted benches crisp on frosted gravel.
dry leaves crunch under unseen footsteps.

Paris

Elm trees stand patriarch
against the violet dark.
Last song of birds
in the birch tree still red
against the darkened sycamores.
Yellow streetlamps deny the light
define the night.

Ham Common, Surrey

September City

September,
season of street accidents
the end of summer loves,
harsh family gatherings,
the death of ancestors.

Cruellest month,
vain anticipations,
false treasures kept in empty wardrobes,
all safely gathered in,
blackberries, the beginning of hollow fruitfulness.

Double agent,
tireless infiltrator,
sunlight on empty promenades,
image seen in a tarnished mirror,
the burning-off of stubble.

September,
season of preparations,
kisses like holiday snaps,
the taste of warm bodies
like mislaid addresses.

September,
time of separations,
tides turn towards the moon,
chrysanthemums at city corners,
children return reluctant to classrooms.

Cruellest season of sunshine and funerals,
mists and ambulances,
bulldozers clearing the debris of summer.

Poems from Germany

" . . . Songs of a wayfarer . . . "

1

Giant hogweed takes over suburban gardens,
unobtrusively,
murmuring of *lebensraum*
VORSICHT BISSIGER HUND
thunders from every gateway,
only the foxglove wanders free;
the evening light
is decorated with oakleaf clusters.

2

Primroses lurk in the darkness of cupboards
the bird has been deflowered, feathers drift
across stained bedclothes. A sad girl
prepares the grave of the last amaryllis
märzebecher   maiglöckchen
the sound of the last train
drowned by the sound of the fountain.

3

GEOFF BOYCOTT we love you
Christopher Isherwood is a fucking liar
written on The Wall
rabbits run free
in the grey Vopo wilderness
body soft in the lamplight
shy voice on the telephone
a small crimson bear
left at Bahnhof Zoo
in the early morning.

4

Perfumdeo/a found poem

Spring dream
Yellow moon
Wild flower
Green summer
Blue river

      (Deodorant names from a supermarket shelf)

5

Dream

The blue dream rises gently from the ground
its pink mouth agape
hovers above the crowd
bumps gently against an ochre dream
drifts towards the sun
which is ringed with rainbows.

                     Max Beckmann, "Der Traum" (1927)

6

You are the tiny onion
given like a pearl
in the crowded lunchtime café
a poem hidden
in the oyster of your smile
while the sun runs amok
in the busy street
drunk on daffodils.

7

I bring you from Germany
tangerine-flavoured lipsalve
called KISS ME
a chocolate hare for Easter
and a pack called, simply,
Anti-Baby Condoms.

8

acrostic

My
Only
Night
In
Köln
Alone.

9

Sunlight on the Alster. A boat called Charly
bobs behind your head. Words left
unsaid. Shade of umbrellas, willows;
a dazzle of green park, thick brush-strokes

on the water. Empty glasses on the orange table.
You teach me to say *zahlen bitte*. Flotillas
of baby ducks. Swans turn, languid as
middle-aged sunbathers, stirring to do the other side.
The minutes to go like the lapping of small waves
as the ferryboat arrives.

(*Würzburg/Siegen/Cologne/Berlin/Munich/Hamburg*)

Three Landscapes, Yorkshire

1

Morning fields
rich with buttercup and fennel.
Mysterious armchairs
lichened to stone.
Your cerise dress seen amongst
rhododendrons
in a viridian valley.

2

The valley sighs blue in the afternoon
cuckoos imitate people imitating cuckoos
chimneys shift from foot to foot in the heat
like traffic policemen.

3

Evening:
your pale pink shirt
the columbines outside the window
the sky above the hill
all coloured the same.

Only your eyes
retain the cornflower afternoon.

Adrian Henri's Talking Toxteth Blues

Well, I woke up this morning, there was buzzing overhead
Saw the helicopter as I got out of my bed,
Smelt the smell of burning, saw the buildings fall,
Bulldozers pulling down next door's wall.
    Toxteth nightmare . . .
        . . . yes . . .
           . . . city with a hangover.

Then I remembered what happened last night
The sirens and the shouting and the TV lights,
Banging on the riotshields, petrol bombs in flames,
Cars all ablazing, shattered window-frames.
    Felt sick to my stomach . . .
        . . . don't cry for me . . .
           . . . Upper Parly.

Saw a busy lying blood pouring from his head,
Saw one stop a paving stone, thought that he was dead.
Heard the sound of engines in the bright orange night,
Saw the headlights blazing, saw the crowd in flight.
    One of them . . .
        . . . didn't run fast enough . . .
        . . . Land Rovers . . .
           . . . long way from the farm.

Well, I saw the Chief Constable up on TV
And the Superintendents, but they never saw me,
Saw the Home Secretary and the Minister for Riots,
And all them social workers who just never keep quiet.
        . . . never met a one of them . . .
           . . . neither did the coppers.

Saw a woman walking in the firelight's glare,
"Hey, Aunty Maggy, what you doing there?"
Arms full of liquor and a portable TV,
Said, "All the rest are doing it, why not me?

             . . . do yourself a favour, son,
                . . . nice music centre . . .
                   . . . just over there."

Well, I thought a bit about it and I took her advice
Crowd was having fun and the goods looked nice,
Then a scuffer copped me and they threw me in a van,
Took me off to Risley and the Magistrate Man.
             . . . exemplary sentence . . .
                . . . act as a deterrent . . .
                   . . . law 'n' order . . .
                      . . Toxteth nightmare . . .
                         . . . city . . .
                            . . . with a
                               hangover.

Colden Valley, Early Spring

Frost persists to afternoon
on one side of this valley
icicles depend
the shadow of the other bank
moves inexorably to the diagonal
never allowing the daylight to fall
here.

Rich textures of lichen
green elephant-hide of beeches
palest sienna of bracken
beckon in the March sunlight.

Here there are only stones of purest marble
frozen in small streams.
The brightest afternoon
cannot dispel the darkness
beneath these stunted branches.

Landscape with Aeroplanes

the sound of a jetfighter
gathers itself across the sky
tears between us
rumbles into insignificance
leaving only our silence
and the housemartin
mimicking its going.

foxgloves reach out, beckon
cow-parsley spread open in supplication
tiny secrets of wild strawberries
known only to butterflies, distant
droning of a tractor, a bird-scarer
regular as the one o'clock gun. Smell
of honeysuckle and the marzipan breath
of meadowsweet, heavy
in the afternoon.

sudden thunderjet

hurls out of the hedge

scattering the rooks who croak
their indignation. Two magpies
flap across a field full of sheep.
distant tors of Dartmoor,
and the sudden apparition of a white cat
at a turn of the lane.

dragging their sound behind them

the jets startle by again.

North Devon

Aubade

I mourn for something that was never there
Remind myself of times a year ago:
The scent of roses in the morning air.

In this small room the senses all declare
You were with me, my love, and yet I know
I mourn for something that was never there.

Mist hides the hills, the season is so unfair,
Left here I sit and watch the summer go,
The scent of roses in the morning air.

Bees can't resist the honeysuckle's snare.
Frantic as they are, clumsy and far too slow
I mourn for something that was never there.

Thoughts of your eyes, the morning in your hair,
Lost like a leaf against the river's flow,
The scent of roses in the morning air.

Time will not stop: your careless hand will tear
The faded snapshot, all that was left to show.
I mourn for something that was never there,
The scent of roses in the morning air.

Poem i.m. P.G. Wodehouse

Darkness at the Drones Club
dust settles silently on mahogany chairbacks
a ghostly footman shimmers in
black-edged card on a silver salver.

From a Hollywood Diary

1

"People used to say my place looked you know
comfortable but I wanted it to look artistic you know
artistic kind of. So I took out the Dining Area
and made a kind of gallery wall . . . it's nice here
. . . you want to go to the beach Sunday? OK
. . . it's a deal. Ten o'clock . . . I'll come by for breakfast
. . . OK?"

2

Marina del Rey:

HOME OF TURTLE RACING EVERY THURSDAY NIGHT
the split white skirts of 1940 Acapulco waitresses.

Beyond the freeway, the sagebrush,
the oilpumps nod, patient as donkeys.

3

dust,
ash from the bushfires in the next canyon
skin the pool. Cacti, succulents,
heaped-up palm trees. Silver-blue,
silver-purple, leaves from the Silver Dollar
Eucalyptus pour open-handed on to my notebook,
skim the blue depths.
Later, the sky shades blue to green, orange to purple
against the silhouettes of palms. Crescent moon
puny against the fireglow, the bright neon.

4

pale sand against the dark-green sea
a lone woman practising Tai Ch'i
the black girl in suntop and cutoffs
rollerdances to music only she hears
from the headset in her ears.

A postcard home: "I've just paddled in the Pacific.
Terrific. Wish you were here." I munch Pastrami, see
REAGAN NAZI painted on the concrete seawall.

sunlight falls
on YE BIKINI SHOP
RENTA-BIKE
RENTA-SKATE
RENTA-BOARD
the blue maw
gaping white jaws
of THE FISH SHANTY.

sandpipers,
head, feet and beaks
going like clockwork,
play chicken with the breakers
like naughty children.

5

cheeky Chicano girls
from Hollywood High – *où sont
les* Foxy Ladies, *Star Magazine*,
Bowie-eyed teenqueens
d'antan?

6

muscular
hustlers
guard
the S & M
boulevard.

7

"In Southern California the Colonel's got more
Than three hundred kitchens with chickens galore."
sings the radio.
                    The old folks go
to Plummer Park, talk of the Old Country, play cards
in summer sun. DOG EXERCISE AREA
empty, cyclone-fenced. Dogs exercise
everywhere else. Blue-rinsed old ladies,
trouser-suits bright as azaleas, hurry in bunches
for their welfare lunches.

8

I loved you, missed you, wrote poems for you here
in 1973. Now you sip opposite me
six o'clock cocktail ritual, Carlos 'n' Charlie's,
Barney's Beanery, The Mirabelle. We do not tell
the times between, sweet and bitter
as a Margarita.

"And tonight . . .

The taxi. The dark doorway. Sudden curtains.
The blinding light. You do not understand.
This poem is pushed into your hand.
The sound of applause. The smiling compère.
The poem is bound between red leatherette covers.
Pages of glossy photographs. Dates, names, places,
some of which you may
have been connected with.
We have flown 6,000 miles at limitless expense
someone you do not remember. We have not thought
to bring the pale-faced girl
who had the abortion in 1964. Nor
the adopted child happily unaware
in Huddersfield. We have brought
the best man you detest
from the wedding you knew even then was a mistake,
we have brought your bride; she is making every effort
to look happy. Showbiz personalities you may have
rubbed shoulders with, or once visited your town, are here.
Their teeth gleam, sincerity teems
like a sweat under the spotlights. Do not fear
this is a happy occasion: the compère says so.
Various elderly relatives are trundled in. The fun can begin
in earnest. He is here, smile at the ready,
the poem held steady. Accent thick
as Irish coffee. Earnest author. Firm announcement.

> . . . gentle reader, this is
> your poem"

Penny Arcade

(for Joseph Cornell)

Utopia Parkway:
Blind arcades. Bouquets
of shipwrecked flowers.
Melted majesty of the sunset. *Salsa verde*.
The city from 100 storeys
open to the night. WE HAVE RUSH
shout the walls, the highways.

Utopia Parkway:
Night tide. Beauty convulsive as
eyes lit by sea-light. Outside
the white hotel the stars
are printed in their course.
666 in neon
above the frozen, haloed city.

Utopia Parkway:
Parrots wait
patient as pharmacists. Drifts of dawn
like ice-floes against tall towers.
Miss Jasmine glitterqueen
declares the daylight,
hearts scattered on the broken kerbstones.

A palace of dreams waits untenanted
A parkway of light up the morning street.

New York City

Angler

His waders among the water-crowfoot,
intent behind his sunglasses, he casts repeatedly,
does not see me pass.
                    I sit
on the riverbank, see the meadowsweet,
agrimony, remembered dragonflies,
hear the water break the channel, cast about
for words.
          Later
he trudges past, his creel
empty, sees my empty
notebook, smiles a secret smile
of complicity.

Totleigh Barton, Devon

A Wee Scottish Song

(for Paul McCartney)

Listen, hen,
there's nae folk in the glen
nae monsters in the loch
och
but it's dull
in the Mull of Kintyre.

Dial-a-Poem

a poem
instead of a phone call
a jewel
exchanged
for a green apple
or an empty station
two minutes
of silence
away from the red-framed world
outside

a song
for a kiss
a kiss
for an apple
an apple
for a jewel
a jewel
for a poem
a poem
instead of a phone call
I didn't make
last night.

Canadian Landscapes

1

Mist and mirrors.

Nude stranger peering round the corner:
the divided self in bathroom mirrors.

Tops of glass towers lost in mist.

Black squirrels scurry among yellow leaves
Storm-windows stacked in suburban kitchens.

Toronto, Ontario

2

Pumpkins for sale at the side of the road
a red fire-hydrant in an orange forest
the rich sienna of peeling arbutus
fields of kale iridescent as eucalyptus leaves.   ,

Grey-pink seatrunks, grey-green water
of the sound. Shoals of islands
bask in the morning
sky soaring towards the Pacific.

Victoria, B C

3

Last night they showed us the sunset.
The prairie sky shading to purest green.
Only the lime-green streetlights
remain. Now
it's the dawn

```
        S
        O
        U
        T
        H
   HughMcColl's
        P
        A
        R
        K
```

coming up like – if
not exactly thunder – an
angry purple line
hard against the red horizon.

Edmonton, Alberta

4

As I walk this motel
the corridors snarl, shake
with the tread of unseen feet. The elevator
mutters "trick or treat".
Grey faces loom
over the shattered ice-machine.
In the gloom of the cocktail lounge
stark muzzles croon
soundlessly.

Regina, Saskatchewan

5

The Northern Lights
rise in the sky, twitch,
descend.
Above
the bungalows
the red steam from an exhaust

the frozen puddles
the huge shapes push
and pull, like shower-
curtains, gently,
gently.

Saskatoon, Sask.

6

LAURA SECORD:
dark chocolates on
a dazzling white counter. A
dark chocolate arm from
a dazzling white sleeve
framed in the doorway.

Yellow lamplight. Two bodies
together on yellow hotel sheets.
Outside, the car brakes, electronic
police-sirens scream
like animals mating.

Montreal, Quebec

7

Huge skies open to sunset,
pale orange of tamaracks,
the sudden interruption of mountains.
POULET FRITE A LA KENTUCKY
armchairs on white verandas
fir trees black against the clear light
fading from blue to green to orange
MOTEL   BONNE CUISINE   COCKTAILS
in the bar Le Georgian Willie and Waylon,
Emmylou and Dolly, sing the night. I wake
to remembered loving,
the dream of a field of dazzling snow.

Lennoxville, Quebec

8

. . . "The storm of embraces,
The circus of dark departures."

Christopher Levenson

Sunlight, and the clear chime of bells
in at the open window. Traces of you
still on the pillow, on my body, in this room
far above the neon city. Mist
and mirrors. Above the glass towers
the clouds have got stretch marks.

Toronto, Ontario

Season Song

love
lies buried
like poppyseeds by a motorway
for many an autumn
cold mists
chance meetings
winters of strangers
snow
drifting through conversations

spring
stirs the ground
words not yet spoken
punctuated by crocuses
horse chestnuts bud
hesitant as phonecalls

summer
come at last
celandines bring swallows
words blossom
like meadowsweet
foxgloves in shaded gardens
tears like summer rain
pavements warm as kisses
eyes in the darkness
mysterious as trout streams

now,
in the warm darkness of you
evergreen and deep as forests
we store these words
against a cold season.

For a Feminist Poet

If I tell you I've gone weak
at your knees
will you promise
not to write a poem about me?

. . . and the days grow short . . .

mid-
September
and already
the poems are starting to draw in.

Souvenirs d'Anglesey

Valse

1

the sea,
and first sight of storage-tanks
early blackberries
and a white goat
grazing on a guest-house lawn.

2

pale moon
in an immovable blue sky

bright Pompeian light
on symmetries of abandoned kilns
votive shapes
of bleached brickwork.

slow
suck
of the tide
perspectives of curlews
and the distant sound of seagulls.

3

double-shaded
rockpools
crimson, viridian
dreams
against slow rhythms
of monotone weed.

4

white sheep
clipped
neat as topiary
three dark-green sandpies
against the sunlit grass.

5

a sprig of weeping willow
from where his brave leg lies buried
in some corner of a foreign field.
Before painted perspectives of a harbour
haunted by sea monsters
the Fifth Marquis (as
Pierrot) waltzes nervously
with one elegant, leather limb.

City Morning

7 a.m.:
I huddle the thought of you to me
like a child's comfort-blanket.

At Your Window

proudly I present
a dead mouse
at your window
dismembered birds
at the kitchen door
cannot believe
do not conceive
your horror
at the gifts I bring you.

Morning Landscape, Tattenhall

Two saturated wreaths of poppies
at the foot of the War Memorial.
Behind the drenched coppice, tiny
waterfall, tangled winter branches,
a haunted grange still dreams.
Over the bridge, and two sudden beams
of sunlight from the broken sky
touch the distant hills,
like an Annunciation.

Tattenhall, Cheshire

Dusk Song

Only to drown in the dark of your eyes
eyes that haunt parsonages
that well like the sea on beaches
eyes as warm as August
as lonely as a cricket pavilion shrouded in mist
distant as spaces between the stars.

Only to know you waiting in the boathouse
lap of sea-light on dilapidated walls
lost child on the moors
crying at the blood on the spotless table-cloth
your dreams filled with nightmares and rocking-horses
as you haunt mine.

Only to touch you in dusty hotel rooms
the busy restaurant, the echoing ballroom,
green grass growing everywhere between us.

Only to drown in your eyes like morning
mysterious as duskfall on distant planets
familiar as sunlight and the smell of seaweed.

Evensong

I write you poems in dayglo colours.
You hold them against the sunset
and tell me you cannot read them.

New York City Blues

(for John Lennon)

You do not cross the road
To step into immortality
An empty street is only the beginning

The words will still flow through you
Even on this cold pavement,
Are heard in some far place
Remote from flowers or flash-bulbs.

In that city, on Gothic railings
Dark against the snowy park
Still a dead flower, a faded letter,
Already one month old.

"Life is what happens to you
When you're busy making other plans,"
This empty street
Is only the beginning.

Here, in your other city,
Riot vans prowl the December dark,
Remember angry embers of summer,
Familiar ghost guitars echo from stucco terraces.

Meanwhile, in the Valley of Indecision,
We rehearse stale words, store up expected songs,
Celebrate sad anniversaries.
Flowers and flash-bulbs. Cold pavements.

You do not cross the road
To step into immortality
At the dark end of the street
Waits the inevitable stranger.

304

Cat

Today, up early for a morning train,
I heard it. Distinct and near.
A thin mewing, as of a cat
locked in somewhere. In my ear
as I ate a hurried breakfast.
Was it your familiar voice again?
I do not know. Know only that
in that high sound the past
came flooding back.

Small and black.
                    Fifteen years,
eight poems, three or four paintings.
Not always at the centre of things: an attendant lord,
perhaps, one that will do to start a progress,
swell a scene or two.

The Entry of Christ into Liverpool
                    You
are there, getting under the feet of heroes, friends
some now almost forgotten. You stare
out of the picture. Banners. Distant sounds
of Orange Lodges. Strange
we never really named you.
                    Left behind
by Fred who went to Canada, and
didn't come back. Fierce, tiny, black,
you dominate the house, allow
no stranger animals within.
                    Polished, O-Cedar

floorboards of our top-floor flat. White brick wall,
brass fireplace. You downstairs, "big-eyed in the hall
for Kit-e-Kat". Like Caligari you patrol
the crooked roofs of Canning Street. Attic bedroom,
skylight that you leap through, surprising us
to morning. Familiar meals, familiar money-quarrels,

gradual separation. The paved backyard she sunbathed in
exchanged for one a block away.

You stay,

apparently unnoticing.

"Black cat
called my
darling on
a spring day"

(H.H.,2.2.1964)

Rose-bay

willow-herb she pressed in '58
given ten years later, with kisses.
Small poems warm as eggs. Rainbow words
written from Rossendale, tucked in bright blue
envelopes. *Holy Night, Silent Night*
. . . *Really Got a Hold on Me* . . . "Glad to be
seen with you" . . . Brown stockings, dark-blue
sneakers, suspender belt. First snow, cold hands
in Piccadilly Gardens. White
Christmas loudspeakers.

Forlorn sound,

a thin high

mewing. Perilous seas,

faery casements.

By the desk,

a photograph,
two frozen strangers. Times preserved
only in poems,
like aspic.

No
madeleine and lime tea
but sausages and coffee
and that elusive noise
again.

1968 and summer gone.
Hands held in parks and palm-houses,
backstage and bedsits,
gone with first frost. All our spring
ending.

Worried letters to me in the USA.
You have run away, come back,
won't eat. She writes perpetually
of diets started and abandoned, hers
and yours. Films she's seen, the *Beano*,
Coronation Street, the house (this house)
we're buying. Crying at being alone.
Long-distance voice on the telephone.
Enormous in your winter coat, plagues of fleas
in summer.
        The freezing fog
that changes Princes Road
into a dreamworld for her. Cobwebs,
dandelion clocks.
        Now moved here
and six months ill. Measured-out tiny meals,
the pills. Waiting for her sound along the street,
at the door, morning and evening, your warmth
curled against the bedclothes at my feet.
Then the time
        I put a child's toy necklace
round your neck at Christmas. Artificial pearls
in the light by the kitchen door. Your face
against the glass. Come in from a party, she thinks
the toad who lives in the grid by the corner
has changed you into a Princess.
        How
you'd pump your claws, relentlessly,
when happy, dribble on people's laps, scrabble
at scraggy plants where lilies last
in the sun-starved backyard bloom'd.

   Un Déjeuner sur l'Herbe her
spread naked across two canvases
above the picnic ham, salami, sliced watermelon.
Derek and me, his black-and-white dog
behind her in a Shropshire garden. Long grass,
lichened stone, a shock of nasturtiums.
          You sit among them
there in the foreground, stare from the picture
again.

               Screwing

on the settee can't wait in the hallway dark-
green Pre-Raphaelite "Sunday dress" naked
beneath the folds, the smell of her, the sight
of white breasts in that green-shaded bower;
glimpsed thicket as she leans above me.
         You,
perched on the arm, watch, unblinking.

             Afterwards,

wet patch on the Morris print, we wonder
what you're thinking.

Now,
the thin high mewing comes again
sharp and insistent as the remembered taste
and smell. What stories you could tell.
Late autumn. Dead chrysanthemums

RELATIONSHIP COMPLETELY DESTROYED
Black November claims responsibility

near,
clear as the sound of traffic or milk bottles.

The humpbacked bridge by her friends' house
where we used to meet. The morning street,
the prison wall, the time a ball came over it,
fell at her schoolgirl feet. Poems in her every
letter. Butterflies in the dark of pillarboxes.
The aching bridge, white platform
of separation.
Seven years since
and somehow still together.
Cold sidewalks of New York,
warm pavés of Paris. Hampstead Sundays,
Normandy mornings.
Shared poems
often for others.
Typewriter from the top floor,
telephones. Summer coffee on the step
by the front door.
You, of course, insist
on sitting on the newspapers
we want to read.
Two years now
since that bright walk in the morning
sun. Going for milk and papers,
she found you. Dead
in Hope Street. Not injured,
not run over, just lying
on the May pavement.
So whose voice now, so close to ear?
What plaintive sound? Ghost cat
shut in what phantom cupboard?

Our morning rituals, wordgames, who
makes the drinks, dream conversations

no longer include
the feeding of you.
                         Forgotten
hangover smell of catfood.

Like summer rain. Glimpsed rhododendrons
from a train. Met in a foreign city,
the last one never knew you. Gone now,
too.

                         No more
panic keys for someone to feed you,
let you out and in.
                         Once left you
locked out for a week.
                         Your frantic squeak
of hunger, welcome.
                         Finish the coffee,
check the key, close the door quietly
behind me.
                         Down the steps, the tiny sound
not quite gone away.
                         Throbs grey the city day.
Dull bell of awakening, distant smell
of burning.
                         A helicopter caught overhead
like a bluebottle.

Not enough fragments
shored up against these ruins:
undisciplined squads of words
riotous assemblies of sentences
hurl petrol-bombs, hack at riot-shields,
smoke looms from blazing paragraphs,
streets of looted volumes. Headaches
hang above the burnt-out cars,
the ruined cinema.

          Pavements
mutter of dole, complain of headlines,
chip-papers.

          Last echo

of that small
voice.

          Memory.

A thin high
mewing.

          It comes,
              again.

And well - are we going
Ehh — well what time is it

Haddock Poem

"He looks like a haddock
it's ALL right."—
For a haddock.

No 71

Billy walker
And his climbing frame
"He limped just down He
Read from me"